ST MARY'S

UNIVERSITY
COLLEGE
Strawberry Hill

A College of the University of Surrey

De Educatione Christiana

THE DECLARATION
ON
CHRISTIAN EDUCATION
OF
VATICAN COUNCIL II

Promulgated by Pope Paul VI
October 28, 1965

Commentary

by

Rt. Rev. Mark J. Hurley

1966
VATICAN II DOCUMENTS
PAULIST PRESS
(Paulist Fathers)
Glen Rock, New Jersey

Nihil Obstat:
Rev. James F. Maher, Ed.D.
        Censor Librorum

Imprimatur:
✠Joseph T. McGucken, S.T.D.
Archbishop of San Francisco
March 6, 1966

THE DECLARATION
ON
CHRISTIAN EDUCATION
OF
VATICAN COUNCIL II

TO
J. K. H

Contents

FOREWORD 7

✠Patrick A. O'Boyle
Archbishop of Washington, D.C.

PREFACE 11

COMMENTARY by Rt. Rev. Mark J. Hurley 15

    I A Text on Education in Vatican
       Council II 15
       Study-Club Questions 24

    II History of the Text 26
       Study-Club Questions 58

    III Argumentum of the Conciliar Text 59
       Study-Club Questions 63

    IV Commentary on the Declaration on
       Christian Education 64
       Study-Club Questions 93

    V Future Developments in Light of
       the Declaration 94
       Study-Club Questions 122

THE DECLARATION ON CHRISTIAN EDUCATION 123
       Study-Club Questions 144

APPENDIX 145

Results of Ballots on the Schema 145
Intervention of Archbishop John P. Cody .. 146
Intervention of Bishop James Malone 149
Intervention of Francis Cardinal Spellman 151
Intervention of Joseph Cardinal Ritter 153
Intervention of Bishop Hugh A. Donohoe .. 156

Foreword

On January 3, 1966, less than one month after the conclusion of Vatican Council II, Pope Paul VI, with his *motu proprio* entitled *Finis Concilio*, reactivated five commissions of this great Council. One of these was concerned with education, and that in answer to a specific request by the Council itself that the subject, so difficult and so complex, be studied further and implemented by a post-conciliar Commission.

No text or document of the Council was really ever finished or completed before the final ballot. Always there was the possibility of amendment, modification and change. The text on education was no exception; moreover, it has remained subject to further development even after the Council: thus the necessity for a careful study of both what happened at the Council and what the future of the text may be. No one in Rome and certainly no one on the Commission believed in 1965 that "the final word" had been spoken or written on education; this the text itself makes quite clear.

"The School Problem" has assumed major importance all over the world, and while there are many common problems, in this instance the differences might seem to outweigh similarities. Since education, and particularly education in the schools, is all but worldwide, education itself varies directly with the diversity of each country, culture, economy and political structure. Nevertheless the Council fathers wanted, even demanded, a statement as necessary for the good of the Church and States as well. The Church, in their opinion, simply could not remain silent, even given the importance and relevance of other Council texts.

The debates on education were very brief in St. Peter's, owing to a shortage of time and opportunity. The danger of a statement too general in nature risked producing only a series of platitudes. Yet the Catholic Church, in Ecumenical Council assembled, did lay the groundwork for future progress in the field.

The Church vindicates the right of everyone, particularly the young, to a suitable education, and a Christian to a Christian education. Parents must remain free from unjust coercion in their choice of schools and their direction of the education of their children. Freedom of education is both external in that the schools must enjoy true liberty in relation to the State and other groups, and internal within the walls of the school itself where the liberty of the Gospel must be the norm.

The Council made it quite clear that the Catholic Church has no intention to scuttle her own schools. Rather, it emphasized the necessity of strengthening the Catholic schools of the world on all levels, as well as the schools of religion of the Confraternity of Christian Doctrine, the Newman Apostolate and other structures of education. On the university level, too, the Council spoke out for true research and freedom of inquiry in the service of mankind in all fields, and particularly in the sacred sciences.

Teachers in all schools, not just Catholic, merit praise for their "true apostolate" for the common good; teachers deserve the appreciation of Church, State, family and society itself, for they are the bearers of the cultural heritage of civilization, and, in the Council's purview, they are doing God's work in their formation and education of the young. The Council indeed has saluted the teacher!

Another bonus awaits the reader of this text, aside from the material and subject of education. This small volume illustrates the odyssey of a single conciliar text and explains how the Conciliar Commissions carried out their roles in relation to the Council itself. Thus yet another side of Vatican II comes into focus, one that is applicable to all other texts, and indeed one relatively unknown to the public at large.

The author, a priest of the Archdiocese of San Francisco in California, is eminently qualified by training, background and experience to offer a commentary. Furthermore, he was a *peritus* or Council expert serving the Commission on Education and most active in its deliberations and its work. He writes from "the inside", authoritatively.

The lively subject of education, constantly under debate here in the capital of the United States, must be the immediate concern of every intelligent citizen, for the resolution of the school question in the United States, as in many other countries of the world, involves the general welfare and the common good of all mankind. Indeed, as the *Declaration on Religious Freedom* states, the test of true liberty is most often measured by the liberty of education in a society.

This small book will challenge Catholics to study and to understand the fundamental philosophy of Catholic education. Such a knowledge on the part of both Catholics and others cannot come too soon.

One last word. The text on education should be studied in the context of the entire Council and in relation to the other relevant documents from Vatican Council II. No document stands alone or unrelated to the whole corpus of sixteen documents produced by the Council.

It is my conviction that this text and commentary on education will be a starting point for progress in this essential apostolate of the Church, for it will be studied by the post-conciliar Commission in Rome, by national hierarchies the world over and, hopefully, by educators, legislators, professional people, members of school boards, parents and the public at large.

✠Patrick A. O'Boyle
Archbishop of Washington, D.C.
Member of Commission on Education
of Vatican Council II

Preface

No text, not even that of Holy Writ or of Canon Law, interprets itself. To be understood thoroughly, any document must be seen in its genesis and through its history. Less has been written about the schema-text on Christian Education than on any of the sixteen schemata promulgated by Vatican Council II.

Some commentators and experts have in rather cavalier fashion dismissed the document without even criticism or a presentation of reasons why they have arrived at such adverse conclusions. The text on education has not had the advantage of much negative criticism, even as a prelude to constructive assessment for improvement.

No one would seriously doubt that the matter of schools and education stands as one of the three or four paramount problems of all mankind. The Church's role likewise has assumed major moment on a worldwide scale. Consequently, this subject cannot be so easily consigned to limbo.

It is my hope that much more will be written and spoken about this matter of education and schools and specifically about the conciliar text promulgated. From the crucible of dialectics and

11

dialogue will come invaluable and necessary assistance to the post-conciliar Commission which will meet periodically in Rome, to the national hierarchies which must implement its provisions, and to the teaching profession and to the entire Church. Education is a live and lively subject in the modern world; the conciliar text deserves a better fate than a cavalier consignment to the archives as a relic of Vatican Council II.

One purpose of this commentary is to stimulate intelligent study and discussion of a subject which can be ignored only at peril to Church, State, family and society itself. The issues are not at all so simple as some have so blithely assumed. Objective, even trenchant, criticism will be a service, whereas silence or dismissal will be a distinct disservice and loss. Only sixteen of an original sixty-four schemata survived through the conciliar processes, and education was one of these elite.

If no text is "self-explanatory", then the presumption must be that "the inside story" would be a most valuable record that would tend to prevent misinterpretations and misapplications of the spirit and meaning of the schema. The dangers of misinterpretation far outweigh the dangers of the violation of Council secrets, specifically on matters special to the Commissions. The Council directive of December 28, 1963, to periti-experts who served on Conciliar Commissions cautioned a prudent secrecy to insure untrammeled freedom of discussion within the Commissions.

This author, using materials for the most part already in the public domain, trusts that he not only has kept within the limits of the directive but also has preserved inviolate personal confidences and committed secrets. At the same time, he wishes to assure that he has written as objectively and dispassionately as he could in the interests of history and truth, but even more, for progress in the field of education and the Church's role therein.

He wishes to express his most sincere debt of gratitude to his own Ordinary, Archbishop Joseph T. McGucken, S.T.D., of San Francisco in California for his confidence and support during the Council, and in particular for appointing him his personal *peritus*, selecting him for the United States Bishops' Press Panel, and choosing him to sign officially as procurator the four conciliar texts promulgated on December 7, 1965; Bishop Hugh A. Donohoe, Ph.D., of Stockton, California, who nominated him to become a *peritus* of the Council and who sustained him in Rome during and in between the 1962-64 sessions; and to Archbishop Patrick A. O'Boyle, D.D., who nominated him as a *peritus* on the Commission on Education and who generously wrote the Foreword to this volume.

Similarly, the author wishes to express his thanks to the President and the Vice Presidents of the Commission, to the members, to the secretaries, and to the Relator and Chairman of the sub-committee on schools, Bishop Julius Daem of Antwerp in Belgium.

Finally, to all those wonderful associates, clerical and lay, of every shade of opinion, who lived and worked and debated and prayed in the shadow of the Council at the house of St. Thomas of Villanova in Rome, a most heartfelt "Ave atque vale".

MARK J. HURLEY

Commentary

I

A TEXT ON EDUCATION
IN VATICAN COUNCIL II

A few months before the opening of Vatican Council II in 1962, Pope John XXIII sent to the bishops of the world the texts of several schemata as well as a list of some 64 schemata which would hopefully be drawn up, printed, distributed to the fathers and debated *in aula* in St. Peter's. It is, of course, a matter of record that the original program was much too ambitious and of necessity had to be curtailed.

Many subjects were eliminated entirely, others were combined, and still others survived the process down even to the final documents which were promulgated by December 8, 1965, at the end of the 4th session. One of these was the text on *Catholic Schools*, combined with the schema on universities, and promulgated on October 28, 1965, under the title *Declaration on Christian Education*.

While no one doubted the importance of education in the life of the Church, yet there was serious question as to whether the Council either could or should speak on the subject. The diversity of conditions in the nations around the world; the vast differences in the operation of Catholic schools; even the problem of the definition of what a Catholic school really is; the fact of the excellent encyclical of Pius XI *On the Christian Education of Youth* of 1929; the Church-State problems in the nations of the world—these and other difficulties suggested at every stage the possibility of dropping the document entirely in favor of a papal encyclical or of action by national conferences of bishops closer to the actual scene. However, silence from the Council on such an important subject seemed unthinkable, particularly in view of the enormous resources of men, money and materiel expended by the Church on schools and education. What would the hundreds of thousands of teachers—priests, religious and laity—think if the Church appeared to take their sacrifices for granted? What of the laity? Those not of the faith?

The text remained on the Council agenda and came to fruition through a variety of influences and attitudes as wide as the world and the Church herself. What *should* the Council say about education? What reasonably *could* it say? Such was the problematic facing the Conciliar Commission on Education.

THE PROBLEMATIC

Perhaps the attitudes and statements on the problem of four very influential groups whose voices were clearly heard in the sessions of the Commission on Education would best illustrate the problematic facing the Council in the field of education. Obviously, each is not mutually exclusive of the other, but the rationale advanced by each can be discussed through the various redactions of the text over the five-year period from 1961-1965.

I *The Preparatory Commission*

For almost two years the Preparatory Commission on Education worked out a text to be presented to the Council. It was given to the Conciliar Commission on Education in 1963,[1] and in the *Relatio*, or explanatory notes to the text, the Preparatory Commission revealed its insights into the problematic facing the Council.

The Council must produce a solemn document on education and schools for three chief reasons: the fostering of education and culture gives a broader field for exercise of the apostolate; pernicious doctrines are spreading everywhere which hinder the free exercise of rights in education; and Christians, because of their ignorance of doctrine, are ignorant of their rights and obligations.

In explanation, the Preparatory Commission pointed out how much sharp controversy had been engendered in every area of the world on the subject of schools, how politics had intruded into the problems of schools, and how enemies had fought the Catholic schools. It stated that, since the Church's schools are in imminent danger, the Church could not be silent. Finally, Pope Pius XII was quoted to the effect that "never as today has

---

[1] The proper title for the Commission is *The Commission for Seminaries, Studies, and Catholic Education* which was charged with the texts of three schemata: "On Seminaries," "On Universities" and "On Catholic Schools."

the education of youth assumed a more decisive and vital importance".

In the view of the Preparatory Commission[2] the problematic involved chiefly a defensive posture for the Church in the face of evident danger, a vindication of rights by law, a view of the Catholic schools as an instrument of the apostolate, and an evident juridical and canonical tone and rationale.

II   *The Emerging Nations*

In many ways the hierarchies most anxious for a strong and vigorous statement on schools and education were those from the "emerging nations". With the rise of the secular State, the position of the missionary schools had become not only changed but in some countries almost untenable. Some States covet the Catholic schools; some politicians denigrate them as relics of colonialism; others wish to nationalize them in the name of "socialism".

Perhaps the description of the President of the Nigerian Bishops' Conference, Archbishop Charles Heerey, C.S.Sp., of Onitsha, Nigeria, best illustrated the problematic facing the hierarchies of "emerging nations":

"In Nigeria, as in many other African countries, the regional governments have frequently expressed their desire to take over the Catholic schools and make them . . . government schools.

---

[2] The Preparatory Commission, under the presidency of Cardinal Pizzardo, numbered in its membership priests from all over the world, but the majority of them were at the time stationed in Rome itself as seminary rectors, professors, etc.

"In the Islamic North, where Catholics are a small minority, the government has been favorably considering a solution along the lines of the system in Scotland, which would give the Church a veto on the appointment of teachers and the right to teach religion.

"In the federal capital of Lagos, a large amount of government control is already in effect, and the Catholic schools have a large number of non-Catholic teachers and non-Catholic pupils, while large numbers of Catholic children have to find places in non-Catholic schools. . . .

"All over Nigeria, government pressure is increasing and the fate of the Catholic schools will probably be decided in the next five years."

What did the hierarchy want the Council to do? Archbishop Heerey revealed the rationale:

"The bishops hope that the Council will strengthen their hand to defend the schools . . . to encourage Catholics to fight for their schools . . . and convince governments . . . that the Church is genuinely willing to cooperate and has a great contribution to make to the education of youth. . . ."[3]

The primary problem, especially in Asia and Africa, chiefly concerned the role of the Catholic school as an instrument of evangelization, as an integral part of the school system of a given country or nation, its support financially vis-à-vis the emerging government and its future.

The hierarchies looked to the ecumenical Council for support and help on what many bishops of the new nations considered *the* most important single question in the Council.

---

[3] Letter in files of author.

III   *Transalpine Nations*

The bishops of northern Europe, where many "Catholic" schools are in reality State schools with close relationship to the Church, or "confessional" schools of Evangelical or Catholic orientation, saw the task of the Council through yet another spectrum. Bishop Julius Daem of Antwerp and chairman of the sub-commission on schools for the Conciliar Commission, presented a paper delineating the problematic of education in the Church. In an incisive analysis, he wrote that the Commission should face real problems, not simply theoretical ones, and determine "exactly the worth of the Catholic school in this moment of history".

These problems he conceived in five theses:

1. The Church, and Christians especially, must assist heroically in building the educational systems of the emerging nations.

2. Christian education is an authentic apostolate and "the People of God" must consecrate themselves to build up the body of Christ, especially the young who will become teachers.

3. Education is a work of collaboration and co-operation among all who have a role in it, whether student, teacher, family, State or Church.

4. Catholic schools must collaborate with other institutions of learning, especially in a pluralistic society. There must be no monopoly of education, not only for the good of the Church but of the State itself.

5. In the field of higher education the Church must affirm the right to liberty in scientific research, and Catholic minorities must consecrate themselves to research for truth.

Obviously the transalpine outlook and point of

view assumed the relatively settled position for Catholic schools vis-à-vis the governments and States of northern and central Europe. Special interest in higher education also reflected an advanced and developed Catholic education. Of special interest was the emphasis on liberty of research.

Just prior to the opening of the Council in 1962 a war of words[4] raged in the press and scholarly journals and swirled around the Biblical Institute of Rome and some of its professors. The ensuing recriminations were duly reported in the press. The fifth principle of Bishop Daem perhaps was a reaction, for he mentioned Sacred Scripture in his explanatory notes. Theology needs, he wrote, the assistance "of a scientific exegesis of Holy Scripture". "Research," he continued, "is impossible unless conducted in a spirit of independence and autonomy. . . . The Church must recognize without any reluctance the rights of liberty in scientific research."

Obviously the problematic of Europe varied in large measure from that of Africa and indeed that as conceived by the Preparatory Commission; it differed as well with the United States' hierarchy's problematic in emphasis and in many major details.[5]

---

[4] Cf. C. Falconi, *Pope John and the Ecumenical Council* (New York: World Publishing Co., 1964) , p. 281; R. Kaiser, *Pope, Council and World* (New York: Macmillan, 1963) , pp. 158ff.; X. Rynne, *Letters from Vatican City, First Session* (New York: Farrar, Straus, 1963) , pp. 52ff.

[5] It must not be assumed that the chief problems and their solutions were confined to this or that group, whether progressive or conservative, translapine or cisalpine, New World or Old World, behind or in front of the "Iron Curtain". Such easy generalizations gradually became blurred and, in some instances, all but unintelligible in light of conciliar debates. One example out of many might be cited on the

IV   *The United States*

What the bishops of the United States desired in the way of a conciliar statement was, of course, colored greatly by the swift-moving events that challenged the stance of the Catholic Church in their own country. President Kennedy's position against federal assistance "across the board" to Catholic elementary and secondary schools, but not colleges and universities, and the practical drive of President Johnson under the anti-poverty program and aid-to-education bill both pointed to the necessity for a clear and viable philosophy of education, particularly in a pluralistic society.

At the same time the very worth and place of the Catholic schools in the United States in relation to the total educational effort of the Church were critically questioned. Was the Church putting too much time, talent and treasure into just one phase of the apostolate? Had not the Confraternity of Christian Doctrine, the C.Y.O. and the Newman Apostolate suffered from inadequate support to the detriment of the Church?

The American members on the Conciliar Com-

---

question of "freedom of inquiry". Archbishop-elect Michele Pelligrino of Turin, Italy, at the 4th session on *The Church in the Modern World*, stated that freedom of inquiry must be encouraged in the ranks of the clergy as well as the laity. While grateful that the calamity of Modernism was avoided earlier in this century, he continued, the means taken were not always in the interests of such freedom: "Such things do not belong only to the past; a few years ago I found a religious living in involuntary exile for having expressed opinions which today we read in papal and conciliar documents. . . . Even in theological sciences many things must be subjected to revision with the progress of research. . . ." (*London Tablet*, October 9, 1965) .

mission on Education were Archbishop Patrick O'Boyle of Washington, D.C., Archbishop John Cody of Chicago (New Orleans during the first three years) and Bishop Loras Lane of Rockford, Illinois. Their voices were heard to express the American point of view chiefly in three major areas:

1. The Council must make a statement that will be the basis for a coherent philosophy of Catholic education, one that will help to clarify Church-State relationships in the field. Freedom of choice by parents to select the schools they want for their children; moral and financial assistance to parents on a non-discriminatory basis; a repudiation of monopoly in education by the State—these were details to be worked out by the Council.

2. The Catholic Church must promote *both* the Catholic schools as such and the other forms of education of those not in Catholic schools.

3. The Commission must make every effort to present a document at once consonant with papal teaching, especially that of Piux XI *On the Christian Education of Youth* of 1929, and also to update that document and make some significant advances beyond it with sound theory.

Thus the American problematic was chiefly practical, but yet not entirely so. Practical conclusions needed to be drawn from sound theoretical bases, particularly if tests of constitutionality were to hold up in court.

Conclusion

All the Commission members, regardless of their point of view or their problematic, did agree that, due to the complexities of the problem of education, the varieties and vast differences of educational conditions within countries and the widely divergent Church-State relationships around the world, it would be essential to propose two "safety valves" to any text adopted.

First, there should be a post-conciliar Commission which would be composed of professional educators and acknowledged experts to build up the conciliar document, which was conceived from its genesis as a beginning and not a conclusion.

Secondly, each national conference of bishops, already envisaged in the text of the *Decree on the Pastoral Office of Bishops in the Church,* should be empowered by the Council to make specific application of the schema on education to their own countries and specific conditions.

The history of the text will illustrate how these various problematics vied for supremacy in the text, sometimes overlapping one with the other, at other times standing firm against each other, and again going down to "defeat" as their ideas disappeared from the document.

Study-Club Questions

1. Briefly discuss the three following reasons for the *Declaration on Christian Education* of Vatican Council II: (a) fostering of education and culture gives a broader field for the exercise of the apostolate; (b) pernicious doctrines are spreading everywhere which hinder the free exercise of rights in education; (c) Christians are ignorant of their rights and obligations in education.

2. How did the bishops of the "emerging nations" at the Council view the problem of Catholic education in the Church? How did the bishops of northern and

central Europe view the problem? How did the bishops of the United States view the problem?

3. Research is impossible unless conducted in a spirit of independence and autonomy. Explain.

4. Mention and briefly discuss three main points of Pius XI's encyclical *On the Christian Education of Youth.*

5. What was the main problem facing the Conciliar Commission on Education?

6. What contribution can the Church make to the education of youth?

7. There must be no monopoly of education not only for the good of the Church but also for the good of the State. Discuss.

8. Is the Church putting too much time, talent and money into the Catholic school system?

9. What are the programs of the following educational apostolates of the Church: (a) Confraternity of Christian Doctrine; (b) C.Y.O.; (c) Newman Apostolate; (d) Y.C.W.; (e) Y.C.S.; (f) Cana Conference; (g) Christian Family Movement?

10. Why are the Catholic schools of some mission lands thought of as relics of colonialism?

II
HISTORY OF THE TEXT

Introduction

No conciliar document can be fully appreciated without some knowledge of the various and labyrinthine paths it had to travel on the road to final promulgation. Indeed, no text was complete or final until promulgated by the Holy Father, and up to the end it remained subject to change and alteration. Last minute additions and subtractions, corrections and emendations found their way into many texts by a variety of avenues, and the document on Christian education was no exception.

Furthermore, this text suffered from a succession and series of "about-faces" relative to its place and importance in the Council programs. Its first title was of the highest category, a Constitution: *The Constitution on Catholic Schools*; then it was drastically reduced to a *Votum*, the lowest category of document in the Council, thence raised to a series of Propositions and, finally, at the urgent insistence of the Commission on Christian Education, raised to a Declaration.

In a similar way the document on higher education, originally a full schema text, was in 1963 cut down to nine short sections and combined with the text on Catholic schools to form one draft, further reduced to six Propositions in 1964, and finally raised to the Declaration status in the final form.

These changes were not a measure of the importance of each text but rather stemmed from administrative necessity and decisions. Originally there were proposed to the Council some 64 separate topics, each to be the subject of a document or schema. Shortly after the opening of the Council it became apparent that the Preparatory Commissions had literally bitten off more than the Council could possibly chew. Hence, drastic reductions were ordered by the Central Commission for the Coordination of the Work of the Council, a reduction ultimately narrowed down to 16 documents finally promulgated after three years of preparatory work and four sessions in Council.

It is interesting to note that Vatican Council I intended to treat of Catholic schools as such in a disciplinary manner, but never had the opportunity because of its abrupt conclusion in 1870. Vatican Council II began with the title "Catholic Schools" but ended with "Catholic Education."

I   *The Preparatory Commission*

Pope John's *Preparatory Commission*, in March, 1962, unanimously approved a text on *Catholic Schools*, which had already been mimeographed in six separate editions. This March text was printed and submitted to the Pontifical Central (Preparatory) Commission which discussed it on June 12 and 13, 1962.

This first printed text stressed the rights of the

family and the Church in education, the importance
of the Catholic schools, and the necessity "everywhere to promote and found" them, the right of
Catholic schools to State support, and the necessity
of both national and international cooperation and
coordination of Catholic schools and universities,
the international center being Rome. The text spoke
of fighting for, and vindicating the rights of, the
Catholic school, particularly "to vindicate the principle of distributive justice in State-aid to schools".

Quite obviously the text was conceived and
created in a thoroughly juridic and legalistic mold,
and it assumed a defensive posture for the Church
in the field of education. Its tone was "negative" in
that it condemned a series of evils under the head-
ings of secularism, naturalism and materialism; it
rejected "coeducation". Even its style breathed
legalism: the rights of parents were described as
*proprium ac nativum . . . suppletivum . . . devolu-
tivum . . . cumulativum*, a litany of juridic terms
meaning "proper or special, natural, complete, de-
rivative and cumulative" and hardly translatable
into English.

Its spirit was expressed in the *Relatio* or introduction to the document, which in its purview saw
education as an instrument for the exercise of the
apostolate on a wider scale and the text as a means
to fight widespread pernicious doctrines which
hinder the free exercise of rights, and also as a means
to dispel the ignorance of the Church's teaching on
rights and obligations in the matter of schools. The
great dangers and threats to the faith and to the
schools were adumbrated even during Vatican
Council I, the *Relatio* concluded.

While there was much criticism of the original
text, as was the case with every single preparatory

schema of the Council, some of its better points were lost over the years of revision, redaction and debate. This text in its first section treated of the educand, the student himself, at length, and also of the role of teachers as such. Both of these emphases were lost along the way.[6]

The Pontifical Central (Preparatory) Commission, after two days of discussion, returned a critique of the text, requiring revision particularly on the rights and duties of educators and on the delicate question of the liberty of the schools vis-à-vis the State. The secretary of the Preparatory Commission on Schools then resubmitted the amended document on July 9, 1962, for conciliar action.

II *The Conciliar Commission*

Vatican Council II opened formally in September, 1962. At its first business session on October 13, Cardinal Lienart of Lille, France, opened the proceedings with his famous motion to adjourn, his purpose being to allow the Council fathers, along with Pope John, to choose Conciliar Commissions which would succeed the Preparatory Commissions.[7]

On December 3, 1962, during the final days of the first session of Vatican Council II, the new members—a majority elected in Council, the others selected by the pope—met for the initial plenary meeting under the presidency of Joseph Cardinal Pizzardo, Prefect of the Sacred Congregation of

---

[6] Cf. *infra,* p. 119.

[7] Cf. *Council Daybook,* N.C.W.C., Session I, p. 31; R Kaiser, *op. cit.,* p 113; X Rynne, *op. cit.,* p. 85.

Seminaries and Universities, with Cardinal Camara of Rio de Janeiro and Archbishop Dino Staffa as vice-presidents.[8]

Education and schools had not been on the agenda of the Council for the 1962 session, and indeed did not reach the floor until November, 1964. Yet the work of the new Commission continued apace over the intervening months. New priest-experts (*periti*) were nominated to the Commission and a new text was approved for printing with one notable deletion.

The Commission in its first plenary session unanimously decided to eliminate an entire section of the original text which treated of the necessity of following the magisterium of the Church in the teaching of the sacred studies of theology, Sacred Scripture and related disciplines. It was thought that a better context for the entire section would be found in the dogmatic Constitutions *On the Church* and *On Divine Revelation*.

---

[8] The Commission on Seminaries, Studies, and Catholic Education, under the presidency of Joseph Cardinal Pizzardo, numbered thirty members: three cardinals, fourteen archbishops, twelve bishops and one superior general of a religious order. These members had a definitive vote in the plenary sessions which discussed and debated the original three schemata on seminaries, on universities and on Catholic schools. These members were assigned to five sub-commissions in which they were assisted by some twenty-five commission *periti* (experts). These *periti* were permitted both a voice and a vote in the sub-commissions as well as a voice and a consultative vote in the plenary or general sessions. It should be remarked in passing and for the record that the *periti* of this Commission were constantly urged and encouraged to speak their minds on the matters freely before the plenary membership, both by Archbishop Staffa, vice-president and active chairman of the plenary sessions, and by the bishops who were chairmen of the sub-commissions.

III *The 1963 Text*

On April 22, 1963, Pope John approved the printing of a new text produced by the Commission, and in particular by the sub-commissions on schools and colleges and universities during their meetings in Rome in February and March, 1963. This document is perhaps the key one in assessing the progress of the Commission's discussions and debates on education and the schools. The title still remained "Constitution on Catholic Schools," the highest category or note. But already the Conciliar Commission for the Coordination of the Work of the Council had advised on January 30, 1963, that the schema had to be reduced to a "brief schema", in view, of course, of the many other texts facing conciliar debate. Particular problems and specific details must be left, the Commission stated, to a Directory and also to the statutes to be found in the projected revision of the Code of Canon Law.

To condense the original material was to run the risk of reducing it to banal generalities; consequently, the Commission chose to eliminate certain sections, retaining them for the Directory or the Code of Canon Law. One such was the proposal to establish the office of superintendent of education in each diocese and give the office juridical status in the diocesan curia along with the chancellor. In this way the "mind" of the conciliar fathers would not be lost to history, a process reminiscent of the famous *Catechism* of the Council of Trent.

The April, 1963, document represented a genuine attempt to meet the severe criticisms of the Conciliar Commission aimed at the original text of the pre-conciliar group. It was much shorter and

strove to eliminate overemphasis on juridic and scholastic concepts. In most cases, it refrained from condemning the host of "errors spreading over the world" of education.

The sub-commission on schools, in its discussion on coeducation, recognized that a condemnation here would not involve most of the world but would mainly concern the United States of America. The "exception" allowed at the discretion of the bishop would actually be a case of the tail wagging the dog, for far more children were and would be in coeducational schools of the Church than in separated schools. Moreover, the public State schools of the United States would by inference be condemned as well. The plenary session accepted this reasoning without dissent, without, of course, passing on the merits or lack of merit of coeducation.

Another item which was to plague the text was the definition of a Catholic school. The original text stated: "That school is perfectly (*perfecte*) Catholic, no more, no less . . . when", following the definition of Pope Pius XI *On the Christian Education of Youth*, "all the teaching and the whole organization of the school, and its teachers, syllabus and textbooks in every branch, be regulated by the Christian spirit under the direction and maternal supervision of the Church. . . ."

While the section did not *limit* the term "Catholic school" to the *ideal* Catholic school, it did define "the ideal"; the same encyclical said: "For, the mere fact that a school gives some religious instruction (often extremely stunted) does not bring it into accord with the rights of the Church and of the Christian family or make it a fit place for Catholic students." Many of the bishops found this definition "too rigid"; indeed, perhaps a majority of schools known as "Catholic" in Europe itself, not to mention other continents, could not qualify under the definition. In most European countries where there are Catholic schools, these are nonetheless State-supported and in various degrees State-administered, even where religion is part of the curriculum and course of studies.

To meet this objection, the new 1963 text revised the offending word *perfecte* to read *vere, i.e.,* from a school "perfectly Catholic" to a school "truly Catholic", a change which gained no support for the document from the dissenters.

An impasse came on the question of the Church's right to teach the so-called "secular subjects". One side argued that it could not be proved from the natural law that the Church had such a right as an original (not derived or delegated) right. The Church as a "perfect" society is known as such by revelation; consequently, to say that the Church has the right to all the means necessary to attain her end (including the teaching of secular subjects) is to posit as its basis the divine positive law. The opposing side appealed chiefly to the encyclical of Pius XI: "Therefore, with full right the Church promotes letters, science, art insofar as necessary or helpful to Christian education, in addition to her work for souls, founding and maintaining schools and institutions adapted to every branch of learning and degree of culture."

Of course, both sides agreed that *de facto* the Church has the right to teach all subjects by reason of other titles such as delegation by parents, the right of groups and associations to found schools, etc. Both sides agreed that the Church had at least an "indirect right" so to teach. Hence the text, which did not at all solve the problem or even push it a single step beyond the encyclical, stated that "as regards the other aspects of human life [*i.e.,* other than the strictly religious], even those pertaining to the natural order, insofar as they help [the Church] to attain her proper end", the Church has the right to educate in all subjects.

It can be noted here that the problem was never resolved in any subsequent text.

Finally, in this text of 1963, the material on universities appeared for the first time, indicative of the pruning process of the Coordinating Committee which ordered that the schema on universities and higher studies become a section in the document on Catholic schools. Moreover, the treatment of Catholic universities as distinct from universities of ecclesiastical studies was dropped; both were included under the simple title "Catholic Universities".

Conscious of the adverse criticism aimed at this text, the sub-committee on Catholic schools appended a paragraph in defense, to the effect that the sub-committee had tried to avoid needless controversies and to eliminate sharp language, and, while defending the rights of the Church, to avoid what might be deemed "a contentious and pugnacious style of expression".

But the effort to meet the many objections which flowed in from bishops and priests over the world, who had meanwhile received this text, could justly be said to have been successful only in a most limited fashion. It was becoming increasingly evident that conditions around the world were so varied and so different that the Council simply could not hope to cope adequately with the problems such diversity engendered. Church-State issues in the nations of the world; the very definition of what a Catholic school is; the role of the Church in society and her rights—all such problems seemed to defy analysis on a worldwide scale.

The hierarchy of the United States, meeting in August, 1963, in Chicago, discussed the school document. Archbishop Patrick O'Boyle, Washington, D.C., a member of the Conciliar Commission on Education and of the sub-commission on schools, presented a critique of the 1963 text. In a positive vein he asked that the hierarchy of the United States support him in his efforts to modify and strengthen the schema by providing a more adequate treatment of the role of the State or civil society as the political arm of society itself in the field of education, a clearer presentation of the meaning of "freedom from monopoly in education" —a freedom which might include Church monopoly —and a better explanation of the question of State support for schools. He also pointed out the necessity to picture the Catholic schools as dedicated to the service of both the State and the entire society in her education of "good citizens". Finally, he insisted that much more emphasis be given in the text to the religious training of those students who are in non-Catholic schools; he asked for conciliar support for both the schools of religion of the Confraternity of Christian Doctrine and the Newman Apostolate for college and university students.

Similarly, criticisms of the sections on universities began to be heard. The sweeping paragraph which suggested centralized control by the Holy See, not merely over the universities and faculties in a general way but even down to the courses of study, caused serious concern: "Special statutes for these universities and faculties approved by the Holy See are to be formulated, by which the whole *ratio studiorum* may be accurately determined; especially, let there be distinction made between fundamental courses and the courses of specialization. . . ."

The "proper method" for scientific progress was mentioned without any clue as to its meaning, and immediately following came the words: "Above everything else, questions of theology and philosophy, especially speculative ones, are to be treated according to the mind, doctrine and principles of the Angelic Doctor. . . ."

In praise of Catholic universities and in an overly generous mood, the text proposed: "The holy Synod decrees that in all parts of the world Catholic universities and faculties be erected which are able to pursue the grave office committed to them under the guidance of that Dicastery [*i.e.*, the Roman Congregation] to which the care of the university studies has been committed, and which shall be given assistance by men truly skilled and chosen from various nations and disciplines."

While it may well be argued that these and other provisions in the text as submitted by the sub-commission on universities were misunderstood, yet perhaps it is more revelant to understand how they were heard by university faculties around the world. In general the reaction seemed negative and adverse.

In December, 1963, the sub-commissions actively sought out the opinions of national hierarchies "which had not yet expressed their mind" on the schema in order to produce yet another redaction.[9] This effort was aimed at the difficulties inherent in

---

9 Cf. Pope Paul VI's speech to the American hierarchy, in audience, Dec., 1963, in which he said: "Tell the sisters of the U.S.A. never to give up the Catholic schools."

the subject; in addition, at the same time, there were gathering other extrinsic problems like so many clouds lowering over the schema. By the fall of 1963, it was apparent that the ecumenical Council was beginning to run out of time. Administrative decisions became necessary, and various documents felt the effects.

IV *The 1964 Text*

During the second session of Vatican Council II the sub-commissions on schools and universities met to improve the document as it then existed, even though the schema was not scheduled to reach the Council floor for yet another year. Reports of the national hierarchies and interventions of both commission members and other interested parties around the world were sifted and evaluated. By the beginning of the year a new redaction had been finished.

Almost double in length, this 1964 version was at once a distinct improvement and something of a retrogression. Many of the disputed passages were more clearly explained and excellent material added, some of which unfortunately never found its way into the final document. Nevertheless, the newest draft reverted to its original defensive and negative tone. The matter suddenly became academic, and the 1964 text simply a relic worthy of study at a later date.

The Coordinating Commission of the Council on January 23, 1964, ordered the schema reduced to a *Votum,* the lowest category of conciliar document. This *Votum* would "underline the importance of Catholic education and the school and indicate the principal foundations on which education and learning must be inspired. . . ."

"Not without some hesitation" the plenary session of the Commission on Education undertook the task. Difficulty arose immediately as to the meaning of *Votum*. Some thought it meant a laudatory epistle; others, a message about education and schools; still others, a list of problems which are prevalent today in pedagogy to be followed by solutions.

However, the Coordinating Commission of the Council had not spoken its last word. On April 17, 1964, it decreed that the schema should be reduced further to a series of Propositions derived from the previous work. In this way the latest text was rendered almost entirely academic; 17 Propositions were printed and sent to the bishops of the world during the summer of 1964.

V   *The Propositions*

The schema of *Propositions on Catholic Schools* was among those schemata which were to be voted upon by the full ecumenical Council *without debate* on the floor of St. Peter's. Therefore, according to the plans, the materials were to be presented as numbered Propositions suitable for immediate balloting, the purpose being, of course, to save time and indeed perhaps conclude the entire Council in 1964.

The 17 theses or Propositions consisted of a foreword mentioning the importance of education and the purpose of the Commission to present "the more universal principles" of education. These "principles" were listed in 6 short statements affirming the dignity of man and his right to an education, especially a religious one. Hence the family, the Church, private groups, and individual men must have liberty to found and direct schools; parents have the right in distributive justice to State subsidies without discrimination.

Propositions 8, 9 and 10 dealt with Catholic schools and the Church's right to sponsor them, the parents' duty to send their children to them, and, although it scarcely followed from the title, the duty of giving religious instruction to those "in schools other than Catholic".

Propositions 11 through 16 treated Catholic universities. The Church explicitly favors higher education and universities which study both sacred and profane sciences and demonstrate the concord and consonance of faith and reason under the aegis of St. Thomas Aquinas. Catholic universities must be resplendent not so much for numbers but in the study of doctrine; all should have faculties of sacred theology or at least chairs of theology. Bishops should care for the spiritual life of students in non-Catholic universities. Catholic universities should cooperate with others in scientific research. Their *ratio studiorum* should be approved by the Holy See, and special care should be taken in respect to mission territories and the Oriental Churches.

The conclusion, Proposition 17, declared "to all people" the Church's willingness to assist the entire human family in the field of education. Its final words included the wish that the new Code of Canon Law would more fully treat the norms for Catholic schools.

The administrative decision to reduce certain schemata to Propositions ready for vote without discussion met with general opposition from the Council fathers when the 3rd session of Vatican Council II opened in September, 1964.

Previously, in February, upon receipt of the directive that the entire schema was to be reduced to a *Votum,* the Archbishop of Washington, D.C., Patrick O'Boyle, as a member of the sub-commission on schools, submitted what he considered the five irreducible points which must be included in the text:

1. The Commission recognizes the importance of Catholic schools in the apostolate of the Church.

2. The Commission affirms that the Catholic schools must serve the common good and a public purpose in society.

3. The Commission believes that a clarification of the concepts of "society" and "State" is essential for a solution of the school question around the world.

4. The Commission calls for justice in the support of schools.

5. The Commission urges the laity to exercise their God-given roles in the apostolate of Christian education, both inside and outside of Catholic schools.

The decision to change the *Votum* to a series of short Propositions further precluded any such treatment as suggested by Archbishop O'Boyle. The appearance of the printed text of the Propositions spurred resistance from many quarters.

The Rev. Edward B. Rooney, S.J., President of the Jesuit Educational Association of the United States, circulated a critique of the Propositions to many Council fathers. His opening comment sums up the matter well:

"If the instruction to the Commission meant

that the Commission was to reduce the [text] . . . to a series of brief Propositions, it seems to me that the Commission has performed the task about as well as it could be performed."

"Under no circumstances," Father Rooney continued, "should this series of Propositions be published by the Council as its statement on Catholic education. They are completely inadequate and they would make a poor impression on the educational world. . . . The section on university education lacks both adequacy and objectivity." Finally, he expressed the hope that in the future Pope Paul would issue an encyclical on education to bring Pius XI's up-to-date.

At the first plenary session of the full Commission on Education, held in Rome in September, 1964, the first speaker was Archbishop O'Boyle. In a sweeping critique of the schema of Propositions, he called it "utterly inadequate". No matter how it would be voted upon, he said, the results would be confusing. If the Propositions were approved, the Church could scarcely defend them; if not approved, the Church would appear to abdicate in the field of education, a most important question over the entire world.

Furthermore, he continued, it was essential that there be a debate *in aula* on the floor of St. Peter's so that the Commission on Education would learn the mind and wishes of the Council fathers.

The only logical thing to do, he concluded, was to write a new text, regardless of previous administrative decisions to the contrary.

The cardinals and bishops of the plenary session unanimously supported Archbishop O'Boyle's suggestion. Pressures were also building up from other commissions to insist upon debate in St. Peter's.

The Coordinating Commission finally acceded to the demands and agreed to schedule "brief discussions" and "petite debates" for the third session.

Meanwhile, in response to worldwide requests, the Commission on Education had agreed to change its title and indeed its point of reference; the schema-text would be entitled *Christian Education,* a term much broader than *Catholic Schools.*

VI *Declaration on Christian Education of Oct. 6, 1964*

In rapid fashion a new, brief text, entitled *Declaration on Christian Education,* was submitted by the sub-commissions on schools and on universities to the Plenary Commission on Education. The major point of difference at this time (October 5, 1964) was the matter of State support for schools. An American view was presented in a special intervention to the sub-commission in these words:

"Catholics by reason of their religion claim no special favors from the State, nor do they lose their rights as citizens. Consequently, Catholic parents and the institutions which serve a public purpose do have a right to equal treatment under the laws of a State: the denial of this right is in itself an unjust form of coercion against both parents and children and constitutes unjust discrimination."

The intervention concluded: "We respectfully submit that the shorter, simplistic and brief statements suggested in previous printed texts will raise more questions than they will solve. What is needed is a much more sophisticated and qualified statement which will allow for proper distinctions, avoiding a doctrinaire secularism on the one hand and an arrogant demand for money by the Church on the other."[10]

At this point the sub-commission modified its view on "subsidies" and shifted its emphasis and indeed its basic thinking in some respects. In view of the parental obligation to educate, their relationship to the State, and the reciprocal obligations between parents and the civil society, assistance should follow the parent, not *per se* the schools, much less the Church.

An introductory footnote to the Declaration also explained why there was a change in title: "Since the greatest part of youth are not students in Catholic schools, it was deemed opportune to change the original title . . . so that the text would treat all schools, Catholic and non-Catholic, and would not neglect other means of education. . . ."

The text itself, less than a thousand words and composed under the most difficult of circumstances, nevertheless presented a good basis for the "petite debate" that would be allowed on the topic in St. Peter's during November, 1964. A new and key provision in the document suggested that a post-conciliar Commission be established to perfect the Church's theory and practice in the field of education, to be applied by the conferences of national hierarchies to local circumstances. Such a provision acted as a safety valve to those who would object to major points. Summarized, the document read:

Prologue: The Council intends to present certain fundamental principles (a) to be more fully explained by a post-conciliar Commission; (b) to be applied to local circumstances by the *coetus episcoporum*. The Council recognizes the major

---

10 Author's record of speech.

importance of education, and its influence upon the life of man and his social evolution in the modern world, and the place of schools therein.

1. Christian education aims at the human and religious development (*perfectio*) to consecrate the world and its natural values elevated in Christ for the great good of society.

2. The Church sincerely wishes *to help* in the field of education in all places and cultures and for all men of all races and conditions and ages; all have an inalienable right to an adequate education.

3. The Church wants to use all means of social communication, organizations of youth, conventions, etc., in the fostering of education.

4. The Church, recognizing the special importance of schools, unceasingly seeks to collaborate in this matter with parents who have the primary and inalienable office and right of educating their children and of freely founding and choosing schools— to the exclusion of all monopoly which is opposed to the native rights of the human person—and of obtaining also the necessary helps (*subsidia*) from civil society. (*Subsidia* here includes money.)

5. Catholics on their part must cooperate with civil society by doing well the work of education and the promotion of excellent teacher formation.

6. The Church strives by all means to care for the religious and moral education of all according to their needs; the Church must care sedulously for the *religious* education of children in whatever school they are found and strive to furnish teachers who can teach religion to these pupils. Parents must realize their most serious obligation to see to it that *religious* education keeps pace with secular education, and we praise those States in which parents

are assisted in this matter of providing for the religious education of their youngsters. (Assistance here does not *per se* refer to money.)

7. The Catholic Church warmly cherishes and favors Catholic schools and declares the work of the Catholic schools *a true apostolate,* necessary in our day and appropriate to our times, and a service to society as well. When and where they can, parents should send their youngsters to Catholic schools.

8. The Church favors all kinds of Catholic schools: elementary, secondary, technical, remedial, adult, university, etc.

9. The Church promotes colleges and universities and nourishes the pursuit of knowledge in the proper method and in the proper liberty of scientific inquiry; these universities are to form truly learned men, prepared to take their place in society and to be witnesses of the faith in the world.

The Council commends higher institutions of learning and wishes them to expand, but rather to excel in quality rather than in numbers; they should give serious consideration for entrance to the poor but bright students, especially from foreign nations.

10. The Catholic colleges and universities should promote the sacred sciences together with the profane sciences and build up faculties for modern research in these sciences.

11. There should be national and international cooperation in the field of education among all schools.

Conclusion: The Church, while professing her thanks to the priests, religious men and women and the laity who have dedicated themselves to the great work of education in the schools, earnestly exhorts

them to persevere in this office so generously undertaken, both to improve themselves in the art of
teaching and in the knowledge of sciences and to
serve and to increase the beneficent presence of the
Church in the modern intellectual world.

Such then was the document finally presented
for the "short debate" in St. Peter's Basilica. Many
of the Council fathers, having studied the Propositions, prepared their talks accordingly, but found
that they were not aiming at the latest text.

The *Relatio* or introduction to the text was read
by the Relator and Chairman of the sub-commission
on schools, Bishop Julius Daem of Antwerp, Belgium, on November 17, 1964. The introduction was
twice as long as the text itself and went to great
pains to explain the tortured history of the text.
Bishop Daem cited the great inherent difficulties of
trying to speak on education for all countries of the
world, and he called attention to the administrative
decisions which complicated the production of the
document. He then confidently submitted the text
to the full Council for debate.

THE CONCILIAR DEBATE,
NOVEMBER 17-19, 1964

I *The General Debate*

There were twenty-one interventions given
orally in St. Peter's on the schema *De Educatione
Christiana* and thirty-seven more submitted to the
Commission on Education in writing. In general,
the conciliar fathers were pleased with the text,
placet or *placet juxta modum* often being included
in their opening lines. All had suggestions for improvement.

The fathers asked that the text itself be lengthened to include their amendments. Several requested that the tone of the entire document be made more personal, more adapted to modern times, based more closely on the spirit of the New Testament, and clearly more in line with the texts of the other documents of the Council and the spirit of the Council itself.

In particular, Bishop Arthur Elchinger of Strasbourg, France, called for "a missionary spirit"; Bishop Paul Guyon of Rennes, France, for "an apostolic spirit"; Archbishop John Cody of Chicago "a pastoral spirit"; Bishop Joseph Dammert of Peru "a pastoral spirit"; Bishop Arthur Rivera of El Salvador, "pastoral and ecumenical"; Bishop Luke Chukwuka Olu of Warri, Nigeria, "apostolic but not proselytizing".

Many interventions called for a statement of the basic foundations for Catholic education. Some asked for a theological foundation; others requested a biblical foundation, and still others, a philosophical base.

Bishop Joannes Pohlschneider of Germany called "for at least a brief theological and biblical foundation" in accord with our Lord's example: "Allow the little children to come to me and forbid them not." In the same vein Bishop Lopes de Maura of Portugal proposed a statement that Christ is the way, the truth, and the life of education.

Moving to the philosophical foundations, Bishop James Malone of Youngstown, Ohio, U.S.A., requested a synthesis showing both the theological and philosophical foundations of Christian education. Specifically he called for a clear distinction to be made between "society" and "the State" and the consequences of this distinction to be drawn out and explained.[11] Archbishop John Zoa of Yaounde, Cameroun, Africa, supported this position. Bishop Hugh A. Donohue of Stockton, California, requested that a synthesis based upon this distinction be composed which would render more intelligible the varying roles and intricate relationships among all those who have a part in education.

Some of the fathers regarded section 3 on the use of modern means of social communication in the schools as weak and a belaboring of the obvious. Others felt section 6 overemphasized parental rights at the expense of others who have a proper place in education, such as the State, the entire community, private associations, teachers themselves, and even the Church.

A group of 168 prelates intervened to say that they wanted a "much stronger statement" on financial aid to the schools. One father asserted: "That liberty is vain if it lacks the means to exercise it." Several asked that the original text basing the claim on "distributive justice" be reintroduced. Another pointed out that enough emphasis was not given to "the parish", and that the whole apostolate of the Confraternity of Christian Doctrine, required by Canon Law, was not so much as mentioned.

Of paramount importance and influence was the intervention of Cardinal Léger of Montreal on higher education. He protested that the schema had been done in too great haste and that the Council fathers had not seen the new text in time for thoughtful consideration of the most difficult questions; indeed they were so tired that "perhaps they

---

[11] Cf. Appendix, p. 149, for the full text; see also *infra*, pp. 71, 111ff.

lacked the necessary physical energy to give proper care to an examination of the schema".[12]

Cardinal Léger proposed that the special office of the Sacred Dicastery (*i.e.*, the Congregation of Seminaries and Universities of the Roman Curia) work to promote cooperation and coordination among universities by instituting and sponsoring worldwide conventions and congresses on selected world problems. Next, he called for a statement in the text that would "prudently but clearly" vindicate the liberty of scientific investigation for universities and for scientists themselves, particularly in the field of sacred sciences. Likewise, he opposed the position of the text on the place of St. Thomas Aquinas in theological and philosophical studies, warning, in an obvious paraphrase, "to beware of the man of one philosophy only".

The contrary opinion on St. Thomas was taken by Archbishop Staffa, speaking in the name of seventy bishops (the parliamentary device to allow a speech even after debate had been formally closed). He insisted that the mention of St. Thomas was neither a straitjacket on research nor an attempt to deny liberty to any theologian or philosopher, but rather a recognition of the true scientific spirit of research, particularly in reference to the relationships between faith and reason.

---

12 Archbishop Peter Veuillot of Paris commented that the discussion came "at a bad time for such a serious subject"; the differences over the religious liberty text and the promulgation of the *Constitution on the Church* and the *Decree on Ecumenism* captured much attention; cf. *La Croix*, Nov. 12, 1965.

II *Intervention of the Bishops of the United States*

The speeches and interventions of the American hierarchy were planned in such a way as not to overlap each other, nor to belabor the same or similar points. Through Archbishop O'Boyle and the *periti* of the sub-commission on schools, the American bishops who wished to speak were each informed of the areas to be covered by other Americans.

The plan evolved into five interventions. Bishop Malone was to lay the philosophical foundations for a solid statement on Catholic education. Cardinal Spellman would present the case for liberty of choice by parents in selecting schools for their sons and daughters. Cardinal Ritter would affirm the necessity for internal freedom within the schools. Bishop Donohoe would draw out some practical consequences and conclusions from the above statements. Finally, Archbishop Cody, as a member of the Conciliar Commission on Education, would ask the Council for a favorable *placet* vote.

Since ecclesiastical precedence determined in large measure the order of speaking, Cardinal Spellman on November 17 was the first of all conciliar fathers to speak on education, followed immediately by Cardinal Ritter. Archbishop Cody was the fifth speaker on the first day, while Bishop Malone spoke on November 18. Although his name was called out on the general listing for two days, Bishop Donohoe was not actually given the opportunity to present his talk *in aula*. Instead he submitted it in writing, and his intervention became part of the official record.

Cardinal Spellman was brief and to the point on one of his favorite subjects, the matter of State aid:

"The direct intention of the schema is to affirm the rights of children and their parents, and not necessarily to seek money from the public treasury for religious schools. In many nations, for historic, sociological and political reasons, the question of school support is a difficult and complicated one."

His Eminence then proposed a formula at once direct and concise: "Parents should be free to choose the schools they wish for their children. They should not in consequence of their choice be subject to unjust economic burdens which would infringe upon this freedom of choice. Since it is the function of the State to facilitate civil freedom, justice and equity demand that a due measure of public aid be available to parents in support of the schools they select for their children."

With a clear reference to the United States' "separation of Church and State" theory, Cardinal Spellman continued: "Moreover, if these schools serve the public purpose of popular education, the fact that they may be religious in their orientation should not exclude them from a rightful measure of public support."

The Cardinal then offered the hope that this formula would help to avoid "useless quarrels" in the future over school aid.[13]

Cardinal Ritter praised the text and emphasized in particular that the Catholic schools, and particularly universities, must enjoy a true freedom within their walls, walls which must not separate Catholics from others or from "life in the marketplace".

---

[13] Cf. Appendix, p. 151, for the full text; see also *infra,* pp. 72ff. Cardinal Gilroy of Sydney, Australia, warmly supported Cardinal Spellman and stated, in his intervention in St. Peter's, that the entire Australian hierarchy both privately and publicly approved. He asked that the formula for aid from the prior text "on distributive justice" be restored.

Bishop Malone addressed his text to a viable philosophy of Christian education. "It is not enough simply to affirm the rights of the Church in education. . . . It is equally necessary to give the reasons why . . . and put in perspective the delicate and complex relationships among all those agents with rights in education: Church, State, family, private associations, schools, teachers and administrators, and the students themselves."

The bishop also made a strong plea for including in the text "the fundamental distinction between society itself and the State", pointing out that the State or political arm of society should be the servant, not the master, of the people.

At his peroration: "We plead, therefore, for the freedom of man in the field of education and indeed as a prime test of the freedom of religion; *dixi* (I have spoken)," the Council fathers broke into warm and sustained applause.

Bishop Donohoe's intervention stressed that the term "Catholic school" not only meant "Catholic" but meant "school" as well, that is, that it should be a school of excellence, of superior quality, and not enamored of numbers at the expense of learning. Neither should these schools be considered "defensive weapons", protecting and segregating children from the world.

The text, he continued, rightly calls these schools an "apostolate", but what of the other schools of the State and private groups? What of the devoted laity who are teachers in public schools? Are they not also engaged in a true apostolate? Do they not take care of the major portion of Catholic children in school? If so, then let the text so reflect.

Further, he asked for more direct participation of the laity not only as teachers but as administrators in Catholic schools. In the matter of research the text must not be timid, for if Catholics believe truth is one and believe the Gospel which says the truth will make men free, then the Church must confidently proclaim freedom of research. Finally, he warned that the text must not overemphasize parental rights to the exclusion of the rights of others with a role in education.[14]

Archbishop Cody spoke in the name of the American hierarchy, of many missionary bishops, and as President of the National Catholic Educational Association of the United States. He praised the provisions in the text for a post-conciliar Commission and for application of the principles evolved by national conferences of bishops in order to meet local conditions and exigencies.

The archbishop stressed the necessity for the Council to produce a text on education because of its great importance, because of the great sacrifices of the laity to support schools, and because of the devoted work of priests, religious and lay teachers. With pardonable pride, he concluded, he would mention the 13,655 Catholic schools of the United States with 10½ million students and 191,126 teachers.

Speaking on November 19, 1965, for the Plenary Commission on Education, Bishop Daem, the Relator (introducer) of the text, thanked the Council fathers for their interventions both orally in St. Peter's and in writing. He took special note of the intervention of the American hierarchy (the only group so mentioned) and promised that "the Commission with the help of *periti* (priest-experts) and

---

[14] Cf. Appendix, p. 156, for the full text of this and other interventions.

lay experts from many parts of the world" would work diligently to produce a revised, satisfactory text.

The Final Text on Christian Education

A Plenary Assembly of the Conciliar Commission on Seminaries, Universities and Catholic Schools convened in Rome from April 26 to May 3, 1965, to draw up the final text on Christian education, as well as on seminaries.

The new text, along with the proposed amendments (*modi*), was not published during the summer or sent to the bishops of the world prior to the opening of the 4th session in September, 1965. The Commission members alone had mimeographed copies; the printing was done after the 4th session opened.

The former text and the new text were printed in parallel columns, as was the customary practice, but where in other documents new words or sentences added in the new text were always put into italics, indicating precisely the changes made, the education text put the *old* words and lines in italics and printed the *new* in standard type. A footnote to this effect was placed at the bottom of the first page of the new document.

The point seemed to be that there was so little left of the original text that the italics might prejudice the fathers against it. Section three affords an example: of its 175 words only 3 terms were retained from the previous text, namely, *parentes, societati civili,* and *ad Ecclesiam.* Nor is this matter surprising in view of the tortured history of the text.

Quite naturally the Commission members feared

a fate similar to that of the document on religious liberty on November 19, 1964, when a group of Council fathers successfully blocked a vote on the grounds that the new text was in reality a new document, not a revision of the previous text. However, the mood of 1965 was most assuredly not the mood of 1964, and such fears proved groundless.

Three "last minute" additions were made to the text: the sentence that "a positive and prudent sex education" be given to boys and girls as they advance in years; "the family . . . needs the help of society as a whole" in education, thus placing *societas tota* (society as a whole) in contradistinction to *societas civilis* (civil society) which appears in the very next sentence in section three; and thirdly, after a spirited debate for two long plenary sessions of the Commission and by a close vote, the inclusion of the name of St. Thomas Aquinas in the section on research in universities.

At this point, there is no need to analyze the final text; the analysis will be found in chapters four and five of this volume.

With the appearance of the printed text of 1965 some significant opposition seemed to be crystalizing against the document. There were "rumblings" among the American, Canadian, French and African hierarchies, but without a Council vote no one could measure the strength of the opposition.[15]

An anonymous document in Latin was sent to many Council fathers; its title was *Argumentum ad Schema "De Educatione Christiana" Renovandum*.[16] Its opening sentence characterized the posi-

---

[15] "Behind the scenes, a certain restlessness in connection with the prospect of a good Declaration by the Council is now making itself felt. Right now it is a cloud on the horizon. . . ." (Bishop Robert Tracy in *America*, Oct. 16, 1965).

[16] Files of author.

tion of its author: "The schema . . . even after its new redaction by the Conciliar Commission, appears to us not at all satisfactory." Paragraph by paragraph it criticized the text as quasi-identifying "education and schools" and applying ideas willy-nilly from one to the other and vice versa.

The anonymous author also suggested that the treatment of schools be put into the text of the *Constitution on the Church in the Modern World* in the chapter on culture. Meanwhile he advised a negative *non placet* vote.

Not at all anonymous was the five-page document of Abbé Michel Duclercq of Paris which was circulated among the Council fathers in several languages. He declared the document to be already outdated, too pro-Catholic school, contrary to the spirit of the Council, a disappointment to those who teach in State-supported schools, oblivious to the fact that the Catholic school is becoming a diminishing element in society, etc. etc.

Pointing to an evident weakness in the text, Duclercq wrote: "There is a misunderstanding of the educative role of the civil society. . . . It does not consist in simply completing, supplementing or protecting the educational rights and duties of parents. . . . The distinction between civil community and State authority is not made in the text."

The conclusion drawn by Duclercq formed a rhetorical question: Is it really urgent and necessary to produce a specific Declaration on this question? [17]

Bishop Robert Tracy of Baton Rouge, Louisiana, asked the same question in his column in *America,* Oct. 16, 1965, suggesting rather that the

---

[17] Files of author.

pope write an encyclical on education in place of the schema of the Council.[18]

However, the mood of the Council fathers did not match that of those opposed to the text. Duclercq's circular appeared to many to be more anti-Catholic school as such, rather than an attempt to improve the text. On the other hand, the bishops who were opposed simply sought a better document, if not by the Council, then by the Holy Father in an encyclical letter at a later date.

The Final Ballots

On October 13, 1965, the Relator, Bishop Daem, presented the final text for a simple "yes" or "no" vote. Of approximately 2,200 fathers voting (the count differed slightly with each ballot), on an average of about 5% of the fathers voted "No", *non placet*. Section 3, on the authors or agents of education, drew 111 negative votes; section 7, on Catholic schools, 102; section 8, on types of Catholic schools, 116; section 9, on colleges and universities, 132 in the negative.

On the entire schema as a whole, 2,096 were present and voting: 1,912 voted *placet*, 183 *non placet*, and one vote was null. About 8½% voted against the text. On October 14, 1965, amid the applause of the Council, the Secretary General, Archbishop Pericle Felici, announced that the text would "be presented to the Holy Father for promulgation in public session, if he sees fit".

---

18 "To do justice to the importance of the subject at hand, I am inclined to one of two possibilities: (1) a post-conciliar statement carefully and fully treated after profound and expert discussion, or (2) a full-blown papal encyclical, updating *Divini Illius Magistri.*"

On October 28, Pope Paul VI, after receiving the results of the formal balloting, 2,290 *placet* and 35 *non placet*, promulgated the *Declaration on Christian Education* in the name of the Ecumenical Council, Vatican Council II.[19]

---

[19] Cf. Appendix, p. 145, for complete tally.

Study-Club Questions

1. Briefly discuss Pius XI's definition of a Catholic school. Is it too rigid? What is your definition of a Catholic school?

2. From whom does the Church receive the right to educate in all subjects?

3. Does the role of the Church in society and her rights defy analysis on a worldwide scale?

4. Are Catholic schools dedicated to the service of society, the State, or civil society in their education of good citizens? Explain.

5. Briefly discuss Cardinal Spellman's intervention at the Council on the question of State aid to education. Compare his "aid-to-the-parent" theory with that of the Johnson Administration's "aid-to-the-child-in-need" theory.

6. Mention some of the about-faces the schema on Christian education suffered relative to its place and importance in the Council programs.

7. Mention some of the rights of the family in education. Are they absolute?

8. What are some of the merits, or lack of merits, of coeducation and co-instruction?

9. Why were the 17 *Propositions on Catholic Schools* so inadequate?

10. Christian education aims at the human and religious development to consecrate the world and its natural values elevated in Christ for the great good of society. Explain.

III

ARGUMENTUM OF THE CONCILIAR TEXT

Prologue

The Catholic Church understands the extreme importance of education in the life of modern man. The increasing awareness of the dignity of man; progress in technical, social and political fields; the relative ease of communications which are binding all men closer together in one family—all demand a more universal education.

The Church has the mandate from Christ to teach the mystery of salvation to all, but she is also deeply interested in man's earthly progress and especially his education.

The Council will enunciate certain fundamental principles to be developed later by a post-conciliar Commission and to be applied by the national conferences of bishops.

1. *Universal Education*

All men without exception have an inalienable right to a suitable education. Young people especially should benefit from the latest progress and science, especially psychology and pedagogy itself, for an education that fits all their needs.

2. *Christian Education*

Those born again in baptism have a right to a truly Christian education as members of the mystical body of Christ. Pastors of souls must accept it as a serious obligation to see to this education.

3. *Authors of Education*

Parents have the serious obligation, first and foremost, of providing and supervising the education of their sons and daughters. The family is the first school, but it has need of assistance from society as a whole, as well as from civil society and from the Church. In the education for salvation, the Church enjoys original rights, but she is interested in the complete education of mankind "for the good of earthly society" as well.

4. *Means to Educate*

The Church is eager to employ modern methods and techniques in the educative process: the catechetical method and participation in the liturgy, as well as the mass media of communication, youth associations and the like, and especially schools.

5. *The Importance of Schools*

Schools have special importance because they bequeath the cultural heritage of the past, develop the intellectual powers of the students and prepare them for life. Schools are centers of friendship, and their work must be the concern of everyone, even the entire community, and especially of the teachers.

6. *The Liberty of Parents*

Parents must enjoy true freedom in the choice of schools; governments must see to it that parental choice be truly free of unjust economic burden in the exercise of this right. The State must protect the right of children to an adequate education but eschew all monopoly of education, especially in modern-day pluralistic societies. All Christians should assist in fostering education of the young in society.

7. *Moral and Religious Education in All Schools*

The Church is deeply concerned about the religious education of those pupils attending schools other than Catholic and salutes those teachers, priests and laity who instruct them. Parents must be keenly aware of this obligation of seeing to the religious education of their children. States which make special arrangements for the fulfilling of this obligation are especially praised by the Church.

8. *The Catholic School*

The Catholic school must be animated by "the Gospel spirit of freedom and charity" to promote the good of the earthly city and the kingdom of God. The Church considers the Catholic school of the utmost importance in present-day circumstances, and she must be free to establish schools on every level.

Well-trained teachers must work as partners with parents to stimulate students to a purposeful self-activity. The work of teachers—priests, religious and laity—"is in the real sense of the word an apostolate most suited to and necessary for our times".

Parents should, insofar as they are able, send their children to Catholic schools and support these schools.

9. *Special Education*

The Catholic school is encouraged to move into

the fields of technical and professional schools, of "special education" for the retarded, and of centers for adults and those in need of social service.

10. *Catholic Colleges and Universities*

By their nature higher studies are to be pursued "according to their own principles, methods and liberty of scientific inquiry". After the example of the Doctors of the faith, especially St. Thomas Aquinas, scholars can come to a deeper realization of the harmony between faith and science.

In Catholic universities, where there is no school of theology, there should be established an institute or department of sacred sciences.

Catholic universities must be noted not so much for their numbers around the world but "for their pursuit of knowledge".

Pastors of souls and bishops together must adopt suitable means to care for Catholic students at State and other universities and colleges by providing centers and facilities for them.

11. *Faculties of Sacred Sciences*

Faculties of sacred sciences prepare students not only for the priestly ministry, but for teaching in universities and for research. Thus they are important for the bequeathal of the Christian heritage and for dialogue with separated brethren and with, non-Christians.

12. *Coordination in Education*

Catholic universities and colleges must cooperate and collaborate on a diocesan, national and inter-national level, and with schools not under Catholic

auspices. This injunction may well involve the
sharing of the results of scientific research, and the
exchange of professors.

Conclusion

The Council urges young people to become
teachers and expresses its gratitude to all teachers
everywhere who "by their evangelical self-dedication
are devoted to the noble work of education. . . ."

Study-Club Questions

1. All men without exception have an inalienable right
   to a suitable education. What is a suitable education?
2. What is the value of schools? Distinguish "schools"
   from "education".
3. All Christians should assist in fostering the education
   of the young in society. Explain.
4. Should there be moral and religious education in all
   schools, public as well as private? What different
   answers are given to this question in such countries
   as Scotland, Holland, Peru, Australia, Poland, etc.?
5. Those born again in baptism have a right to a truly
   Christian education as members of the mystical body
   of Christ. What is a suitable Christian education?
6. The family is the first school, but it has need of
   assistance from society as a whole, as well as from
   civil society and from the Church. Briefly discuss
   these needs.
7. What is the value of faculties of sacred sciences?
8. How can Catholic universities cooperate and collaborate on a diocesan, national and international
   level with non-Catholic universities?
9. From whom does the Church have the right to teach
   the mystery of salvation?
10. Is a Catholic parent free to send his child to a
    school that is not a Catholic school?

IV

COMMENTARY ON THE DECLARATION ON CHRISTIAN EDUCATION

The Council, through its Conciliar Commission on Education, has studied the entire field of education and not simply Catholic education or Catholic schools; it has chosen certain fundamental themes and concepts considered appropriate to the world of today and in the spirit of the *aggiornamento* of the Council itself.

Vatican Council II has made no pretense that this statement is complete or even remotely a survey of educational problems of importance throughout the world. Rather, the Council has underscored the capital necessity of education for all men, not only as individuals to realize their human potential, but also for the welfare of families, nations, the family of nations and world peace itself. Nor is the role of education in the eternal salvation of men neglected.

The very fact that the document in its opening paragraphs called for a post-conciliar Commission to continue research and investigation in the field of schools and education illustrates the point further. In a similar way the injunction to national conferences of bishops to make specific applications in each country suggests the incompleteness of the text and the Commission's ready recognition of the fact.

What then are some of the most important themes and principles in the text? What are some of the "surprises" in view of the original problematic subscribed to by Commission members, the interventions of the Council fathers *in aula* in St. Peter's Basilica, and the votes cast pro and con and *juxta modum*? (A "juxta modum" vote meant that the conciliar father voted "yes", but with certain qualifications which he submitted in writing.) By implication, at least, the final section of this book, which looks to the future with suggestions for progress in the field of education, will contain specific criticisms of the major lacunae and weaknesses of the text.

THE MAJOR THEMES

I *Church at Service of All Men in Field of Education*

The Catholic Church holds in her purview all men, not merely her own communicants, and she also sees her own efforts and work in the field of education as a *true service* to all men.

The *Constitution on the Church* described the Church as a "sacrament of the world" bound to be totally at the service of men and mankind; as this "sacrament" or sign to the world, her only measure is that in which she serves humanity. Similarly, the *Decree on the Pastoral Office of Bishops in the Church* pictured the bishops as those who "stand in the midst of their people as those who serve". In the same vein the *Declaration on Christian Edu-*

cation specifically enjoins Catholics to *serve* all men, all families, their nations and communities, and to strive for the welfare of all children and all schools, not only because the salvation of souls, which is the Church's special mission, is involved in education, but also "for the good of earthly society and for the building of a better world".

Thus the spirit and tone of this document is *unselfish and disinterested*, outgoing and outgiving: "All men of every race, condition and age, since they enjoy the dignity of a human being, have an inalienable right to an education that is in keeping with their ultimate goal, their ability, their sex and the culture and tradition of their country. . . ." (n. 1).

All children have a right to their cultural heritage; Christians, by the same token, have a right to a Christian education. Those who serve children in this high office and purpose share in a special way in a true apostolate, whether they teach in public or private schools. The religious or other bona fide schools serve not only families but also the entire community, the nation and even all mankind.

Special praise is given to those teachers and those communities and States which, in the "pluralism of contemporary society" and "respecting religious freedom", assist families in facilitating moral and religious training of all youngsters (n. 7). Likewise, praise is given to those Catholic schools which receive non-Catholic boys and girls as students, especially in the new emerging nations (n. 9).

Nor does the Church wish her own schools to be narrowly sectarian, to be bastions and fortresses of protection against the "outside" world, much less ghettos fostering the growth of pupils as so many hothouse plants sheltered and protected from "the madding crowd's ignoble strife". Rather, the Catholic schools internally are to be truly Christian and Catholic, "animated by the Gospel spirit of freedom and charity . . . open to the conditions of the contemporary world . . . to promote efficaciously the good of the earthly city and [to prepare students] for service in the spread of the kingdom of God so that . . . they become, as it were, a saving leaven in the human community" (n. 8).

The document strongly affirms that all education, and particularly Catholic education both within and without the Catholic schools, must be a true apostolate of unselfish service.

Similarly, on the college and university level, an openness of tone and theme affirms the autonomy of individual subjects and disciplines (n. 11), the necessity of collaboration and cooperation with all other universities (n. 12), and the necessity of "liberty of scientific inquiry" (n. 10), especially in the study of sacred sciences (n. 11).

Conscious of the present-day world, the Council enjoins Catholics to be part and parcel of it in the field of education in order "to contribute to the good of the whole of society" (n. 2) and be "a saving leaven in the human community".

The "siege mentality" is not the Catholic mentality.

II *Interdependence, Harmony and Cooperation Necessary among Those Responsible for Education*

The *Declaration on Christian Education* attempts to probe more deeply and to put into clearer perspective the delicate and complex relationships among those endowed with rights and duties in education: the family, private associations, schools, the civil society, the Church, the teachers and administrators, society itself and the pupil-educand. Each has a proper and legitimate interest in education, but within the limits of his or its own competence.

Catholics have often been accused, and not without some justice, of overemphasizing the rights of parents in education to the exclusion of almost all other agents, or of assuming that, when they have strongly affirmed parental rights, very little else need be spoken.

The conciliar document most clearly and forcefully affirms the rights of parents—all parents, that is, and not simply Catholic parents—with regard to education in its most general and widest sense (n. 3), in the free choice of schools (n. 6), and in cooperation formally as partners with the teachers "in every phase of education" (n. 8). However, the text goes even further.

First and foremost, the schema vindicates the right of the pupil-educand to an appropriate education (n. 1). Education and good teaching further involve the stimulation to self-activity in the educand; knowledge is not poured into a student like oil into an automobile. Neither is knowledge an assortment of neat packages to be opened on demand. Schools and teachers must strive to attain self-activity in the educands "to stimulate [them] to act for themselves" (n. 8).

Secondly, the school is a center where those responsible for education often meet and exercise their various roles, hopefully in a spirit of harmony and cooperation and in the realization of mutual interdependence. The teacher is not simply a legate of the family, or an employee of the State, or a representative of the Church, or an agent for private civic or cultural groups, or the perpetuator of the community culture in the name of the entire society. In many ways a teacher is and can be all or most of these.[20]

The school and the work of education, therefore, "must be shared together by families, teachers and associations of various types that foster cultural, civic and religious life, as well as by civil society and the entire human community" (n. 5). Education involves the entire society (n. 3) and demands by its very nature a recognition of the complex interdependence of all involved; it solicits both an intelligent harmony and a willing cooperation among all those with a proper role to play.

On this fundamental point of the interdependence and interlocking relationships of those with a role in education, the text did not in its final form

---

[20] Cf. Bishop Elchinger, *Conciliar Intervention*, Nov. 17, 1964: "Teachers indeed hold the place of parents, but not in everything they do. They receive a mandate from them. But teachers are also vicegerents of society, *i.e.*, of the human community, insofar as it is the day-to-day heir of the cultural heritage which past generations have accumulated."

Cf. Francis Canavan, "The School: Whose Is It?" in *America* (Aug. 15, 1964), p. 154: "We must stop thinking of the school simply as an agent or an instrument of the State or the Church or the parents of the pupils. . . . The reason is that none of these institutions—the State, the Church, the family—is an educational institution in the full sense of the term." Cf. also Pope Paul VI, Address of Aug. 28, 1964, *The Pastoral Ministry of the Secondary Schools* (N.C.W.C., Sept. 22, 1964), in which he asked that Catholics give to the schools "the utmost interest and the most enlightened and selfless service. . . . This is to be said for the school in general, and chiefly for that set up by the State, which is, beyond compare, the most highly developed in its organizational structure and the most frequently attended—and thus the one most in need of devoted, judicious and excellent pastoral care".

enunciate it as clearly and as forthrightly as called for by some Council fathers. Bishop Peter Birch of Ossory, Ireland, for example, stated plainly that, although the text affirmed the role of the parent to be *maximi momenti* (of the highest importance), "this does not suffice". Bishop Donohoe of Stockton, California, dryly remarked in his intervention: "We cannot combat monopoly in education by the State or the government by simply affirming a monopoly of the parents or the family."

While these ideas are found in the text, they are not expressed in a coherent synthesis, a weakness which stemmed from a more fundamental one, namely, the reluctance of the Commission itself to elucidate at proper length and depth the basic distinctions between society on the one hand and the State and government on the other.[21]

III   *Toward a Viable Philosophy*

It is not sufficient simply to affirm the rights and duties of family, Church, State and others in education; it is equally necessary to give the reasons *why* rights and duties are what they are in order to present both a theological and philosophical foundation for the answers given in the *Declaration on Christian Education*. The clear mandate of our Lord to "teach all nations" furnishes a theological fundament on the things that pertain to salvation; however, the philosophical base is not so evident.

The Conciliar Commission adopted as one of its purposes to try to develop further the great encyclical of Pope Pius XI, *Divini Illius Magistri* ("On the Christian Education of Youth") of 1929 and

[21] Cf. *infra*, pp. 113ff.

Pope Pius XII's Christmas Allocutions of 1941, 1942 and 1944, wherein he distinguished between society, which is a *social* concept, and the State (*stato di diritto*) or the juridic order, a *political* concept and much narrower in extension.

Society, often loosely described as "the people" or "we the people", has wider interests than the State or "*civil* society whose role is to direct what is required for the common temporal good" (n. 3). Thus the State is the *instrument* of society, not its master, and the scope of its instrumentality must be determined by the people or society itself. Properly speaking, therefore, the State is *not* a teacher, much less an official interpreter of religion, art, science, literature, culture, etc. The State has rights in education, particularly to pass compulsory education laws, to set minimum standards for schools and teachers, and to require a certain education for citizenship and the common temporal welfare.

With this background the Commission (n. 3) used two phrases in contradistinction: *totius societatis* (society as a whole) and *societati civili* (civil society) or the State, and later (n. 5) "civil society" and "the entire human community".

Thus a basic premise was laid, and, incidentally, a short step by way of development of the teaching of Pius XI, for a viable philosophy and fundamental reason why the Church opposes *all* school monopoly and affirms the right of parents to equal treatment under civil law and policy.

Monopoly in education, which, particularly in a pluralistic society, would be contrary to the expressed will of the people, "is opposed to the native rights of the human person, to the development and spread of culture, to the peaceful association of citizens. . . ." (n. 6).

In the same way, responsive to the will of the people, the text calls for equitable treatment by the State, *i.e.*, the political arm of the people, to accord parents true freedom of choice of schools for their children. "The government . . . must see to it, in its concern for distributive justice, that public assistance is given in such a way that parents are truly free to choose according to their conscience the schools they want for their children" (n. 6) .

It is to be noted that the text does *not* call for aid to schools as such, much less for Catholic schools which are not mentioned until section 8. Help should be given parents to fulfill their duty in education, whether these parents be Catholic, Protestant, Jewish, Moslem, Buddhist, secularist or agnostic, on an equitable basis which will not place unjust or inequitable financial burdens on families.

Schools should be the recipients of aid according to the expressed will of the people, especially the parents. By curious coincidence, as the Council worked to evolve a clear philosophical basis for the vindication of parental rights around the world, the Congress of the United States voted into law an "aid to the child-in-need" theory rather than an "aid to the school" theory under both the Anti-Poverty Program and Federal Aid to Education. Similarly, within the past few years many states in the United States have granted funds directly to high school graduates entering the college of their choice, in a fashion similar to the G.I. bill but, more significantly, based not on a theory of reward or recompense for military service in time of war, but simply where true need is shown and in the interest of the common good of all.[22]

---

[22] During the years the Council was in session (but not necessarily because of that fact) fundamental changes were

The formula for aid to parents in their choice of schools represents not so much a compromise of views but rather a compounding or combining of them. The formulas proposed by the Americans on the Commission were in response to the Preparatory Commission's absolute and unqualified demand for complete parity in the allocation of funds between private schools and State schools in the name of distributive justice. To American eyes the demand was "a dreadful oversimplification of a complicated issue" which would seriously prejudice the position of the Catholic schools in the United States and elsewhere.

The substitute formula, also American in origin, read: "The principle of distributive justice demands that the government, in distributing burdens and benefits within the community, should have in view the needs, merits and capacities of various groups of citizens in general. This principle should control the action of the government in the question of the support of schools.

"The principle of distributive justice would require that a proportionately just measure of public support should be available to such schools as serve the public cause of popular education, whether

---

being made in the matter of State support for non-public schools. In Australia, for example, the federal government initiated a program of loans to schools, then grants for the building of science buildings, and in 1965 funds for the construction of school buildings for "independent schools". Several of the Australian States have established scholarship programs for students, applicable to the independent schools, and have offered to assist in the financing of construction by paying the interest on construction costs. In Peru, in 1965, the national legislature voted into law a system whereby the State will pay the salaries of all lay teachers (not of sisters, brothers or priests) in schools conducted by the Churches and by independent associations.

these schools be religious in their orientation or not."

But having offered a substitute a great deal better than the sharp demands of the original, the American delegates had second thoughts. What was needed was a much more sophisticated and qualified statement which would avoid on the one hand a doctrinaire secularism (by succumbing to those who would deny any help to the schools), and, on the other, an arrogant demand by Catholics for tax money.

The result was the formula enunciated *in aula* by Cardinal Spellman on Nov. 17, 1964. He asked tax money neither for schools directly, nor for Catholic schools; neither did he mention "distributive justice". Rather, in the name of freedom of education he asserted that States must grant "a due measure of public aid" to parents when they select schools.[23]

In section 5 of the *Declaration on Religious Freedom*, promulgated by Pope Paul VI on Dec. 7, 1965, the Council fathers struck the same note on the matter of freedom of choice and freedom from unjust economic burdens in reference to families and parents:

"The family, since it is a society in its own original right, has the right freely to live its own domestic religious life under the guidance of parents. Parents, moreover, have the right to determine, in accordance with their own religious beliefs, the kind of religious education their children are to receive. Government, in consequence, must acknowledge the right of parents to make a genuinely free choice of schools and of other means of education, and the use of this freedom of choice is not to be made a

---

[23] Cf. *supra*, p. 51.

reason for imposing unjust burdens on parents, whether directly or indirectly. Besides, the rights of parents are violated if their children are forced to attend lessons or instructions which are not in agreement with their religious beliefs, or if a single system of education, from which all religious formation is excluded, is imposed on all."

It is to be noted here that the theme of freedom of choice for parents and of assistance for them and not for schools *per se* is consonant with the *Declaration on Christian Education*. Similarly, the strictures on "forced attendance" extend to ideological indoctrination as well as to religious indoctrination contrary to parental choice.

Archbishop George Beck of Liverpool, in his intervention in St. Peter's, maintained that the Church must more forcefully defend the rights of parents in the natural law and show herself as a defender not only of the Catholic family, but of the non-Catholic family as well, by indicating the rights of parents to found and support schools, since all are citizens in the fullest sense and under "distributive justice" have the right to equal treatment. He noted that "in England, Scotland, Ireland and Holland, and in other parts of the world, governments acknowledge the rights of parents and religious schools".

Many other bishops also called for "distributive justice", including those of France, Nigeria, Germany and Latin America. The final text contained the phraseology "in its concern for distributive justice", but only partially included the necessarily complex formula proposed by the Archbishop of New York in solution of a truly complex problem.

The answers to both the problem of monopoly in education and the problem of a just and equitable share of assistance to parents, even as in the previous question of those with roles in education, rest again on the basic distinction of society and the State, the confusion of which has consistently vexed those seeking a viable philosophy of education in the present-day world.[24]

IV *The Direct Educational Work of the Church*

In the past three years a debate, at times somewhat acrimonious, has ebbed and flowed back and forth in the United States, Africa, Latin America and elsewhere as to the relative merits of the Catholic school, the vast investment of time, talent and money put into them, the large majority of Catholic students in State schools on all levels and the effectiveness of the Confraternity of Christian Doctrine, the Newman Apostolate and other groups in the total picture of the efforts of the Catholic people. Should there be a radical phasing-out of Catholic schools in favor of a newer approach to the apostolate of the Church? The Council addressed itself to these questions, leaving the detailed application to each hierarchy and country.

The right to proclaim the mystery of salvation to all men rests firmly on the mandate of Christ to teach all nations (Prologue), and the Church does so both *inside* the Catholic schools and *outside* of them. Her mandate so to teach extends to all her children, no matter where they are or what schools they attend (n. 7). Pastors are reminded of "their most serious obligation to see to it that all the faithful, but especially the youth who are the hope of the Church, enjoy this Christian education" (n. 2).

---

[24] Cf. *infra,* pp. 112ff.

Priests and laymen are strictly enjoined to teach "the doctrine of salvation . . . and provide spiritual aid in every way the times and conditions allow" (n. 7).

Moreover this religious education must be a "quality education", keeping pace *at all levels* with secular education, an injunction taken directly from *Pacem in terris*.[25] Special praise is given to those communities and States which respect this religious freedom, particularly in a pluralistic society, by providing opportunities for religious education (n. 7).

So far, so good! But what in practice?

1. *Religious Apostolate Outside Catholic Schools*

In his intervention, Bishop Joseph Dammert of Peru pointed out the disparity between the Church's efforts *inside* and *outside* her own schools. The large number of priests, religious and laity committed to the Catholic schools contrasts sharply with the much smaller number of those engaged in the religious education of those Catholic children in State schools. "Our organization of our institutions of learning is plainly unequal and indeed partial." Can we continue following this traditional system? Should we hand our schools over to the State? Or can we attempt to take care of both those inside and out? This last option was the choice of the Council.

All Christian children by reason of their baptism have a right to a Christian education "to the mature measure of the fullness of Christ. . . . Therefore, this sacred Synod recalls to pastors of souls their most serious obligation to see to it that all the faithful, but especially the youth who are the hope of the

---

25 Cf. *Pacem in terris*, n. 153.

Church, enjoy this Christian education" (n. 2). This general principle makes no mention of such an education being inside or outside a Church school; obviously it applies to all.

In specific application to State and private schools other than those conducted by the Catholic Church, the text declares that "the Church must be present with her own special affection and help for the great number who are being trained in schools other than Catholic" (n. 7). Students themselves, teachers, priests and laity alike must bring witness of Christ to these schools. Teachers must be found to give the students "the doctrine of salvation in a way suited to their age and circumstances and provide spiritual aid in every way the times and conditions allow" (n. 7).

Here then is an explicit charter for the Confraternity of Christian Doctrine, for its "schools of religion". Although the members of the American Commission had requested specific mention of the C.C.D. and the Newman Apostolate, it did not find its way into the text. Curiously, however, the C.C.D. is specifically mentioned and explicitly sanctioned in the text of the *Decree on the Pastoral Office of Bishops in the Church* (n. 30), as well as in the Code of Canon Law.

The schema goes further: taking an idea expressed in *Pacem in terris*, it asks that religious education be kept up to the level of secular education and Christian formation to the same degree as other formation (n. 7). Finally, the text praises those States and governments which, "bearing in mind the pluralism of contemporary society and respecting religious freedom", assist families in this religious education.

Such praise, of course, runs quite counter in spirit to the famous McCollum decision of the United States Supreme Court in 1947 which outlawed the teaching of religion, before or after public school hours, within the public school building. The Council implies that *some* arrangements should and indeed must be made in the name of religious freedom in every country of the world. It is to be noted that here the Church is defending the right of *all* families "to their individual moral and religious principles", and not just those of Catholic families.

Moving to the realm of higher education, the Council shows equal concern for college and university students. While the Newman Apostolate, and indeed the Catholic Youth Organization, the Young Christian Students, and a host of others are not mentioned by name, they do receive the mandate of the Council:

"Solicitous for the spiritual formation of all their children, they [bishops and pastors] must see to it, after consultations among bishops, that even at universities that are not Catholic there should be associations and university centers under Catholic auspices in which priests, religious and laity, carefully selected and prepared, should give abiding spiritual and intellectual assistance to the youth of the university" (n. 10).

Perhaps the most significant phrase is "after consultations among bishops", which implies that the matter of the Newman Apostolate, to cite one case, demands cooperation *among* dioceses, and indeed must concern the national conferences of bishops as a body. Splendid isolationism will not solve the problem either on a parochial or on a diocesan level.

The work of the C.C.D., the Newman foundations and other associations for religious formation stands as a true and necessary apostolate, strongly sanctioned by the extraordinary magisterium of the Church, in Council assembled. There is nothing "second-rate" about this work; it is not subordinate to the apostolate of the Catholic schools. Indeed, since it concerns more youngsters and students by far than the Catholic schools and universities have under their care, this apostolate urgently needs more attention, care and support from the Church.[26]

But the purview of the Council, even as that of the C.C.D., goes beyond pupils and students in schools and extends to adults as well. Special schools and classes for adults are to be established and promoted:

". . . great importance is to be attached to those [schools] which are required in a particular way by contemporary conditions such as . . . centers for educating adults and promoting social welfare. . . ." (n. 9).

A parallel emphasis is to be found in the text of the *Decree on the Pastoral Office of Bishops in the Church* which points out the importance of catechetical instruction, enjoining bishops to see to it that "catechetical instruction . . . be given with sedulous care to both children and adolescents, youths and adults", including the study of "Sacred Scripture, tradition, the liturgy, magisterium and life of the Church" (n. 14).

The Council would have it that a full religious education program consonant with each one's age

---

[26] Cf. *infra*, pp. 97ff. Many observers think that the "parish" must be given more attention as an educating agency not only for students but adults as well. The text did not treat the "parish" *per se*.

be the primary duty of the pastor; and by implication, this would check the tendency to make the parish excessively "child-centered".

The Council text strives to effect something of a balance between the traditional forms of the apostolate and the exigencies of the present day. But it was not willing, either, to slacken support for the Catholic schools themselves.[27]

2. *Religious Apostolate within the Catholic Schools*

What, then, of the Catholic schools running from the nursery and kindergarten through university and graduate school? Are they worth the enormous concentration of time, talent, trouble and effort lavished upon them in countries all over the world? Would not the Church's resources be better expended and her clergy, religious and laity better employed in favor of newer methods, 20th-century methods, perhaps even to the phasing-out of many schools or donating them to the State?

These are most serious questions, and most seriously argued on every continent. "Plainly unequal and evidently partial" treatment is not a vain or fatuous claim. The Council replies unequivocally, yet without getting into the heart of the controversy which revolves about the amount of concentration and the measure of commitment in manpower and materiel.

The Council leaves no doubt as to its mind:

---

[27] Paul-Joseph Hoffer, Superior General of the Society of Mary and a member of the Conciliar Commission on Education, wrote in *Circulaire* No. 32, Dec. 8, 1965, "The Pastoral Role of Christian Schools," that "it would be erroneous to sacrifice the Christian school to evangelize the pupils in the public schools. The two sectors must be organized . . . in a pastoral plan of cooperation established by the conferences of bishops" (p. 1029).

"Since, therefore, the Catholic school can be such an aid to the fulfillment of the mission of the People of God and to the fostering of the dialogue between the Church and mankind to the benefit of both, it [the Catholic school] retains, even in our present circumstances, the utmost importance . . . and contributes in the highest degree to the protection of freedom of conscience and the rights of parents, as well as to the betterment of culture itself" (n. 8).

The Catholic school is a service to all society, therefore, and its work a true ministry to mankind. "The work of these teachers [priests, religious and laity in Catholic schools], this sacred Synod declares, is, in the real sense of the word, an apostolate most suited to and necessary for our times and at the same time a true service offered to society" (n. 8).

Not only for the good of the Church, therefore, but also for the good of society itself, for its religious freedom, its cultural heritage, and in the protection of parental rights, the Catholic schools are a service to all. Moreover, they constitute a true apostolate suited to modern times and conditions.

In two places the term "subsidiarity" appears. The State is enjoined to supply education where parents or other groups fail, "according to the principle of subsidiarity" (n. 3). The principle asserts that the State in general may not assume functions which citizens either alone or in groups and associations can do as well or better. The text unfortunately takes a very much narrower view in section 3 and grants the State power only *in defectu parentum* (when parents fail in their duties), whereas the principle applies even when there is no such defection. In section 6 the principle is also invoked, properly, against monopoly of schools by State, Church or private groups.

The point is not well expressed in the text, but the idea underlying "subsidiarity" seems to be that the Catholic schools, by their very existence, constitute a bulwark against monopoly not only of education but also of culture, and against any denial of religious liberty. The Council's *Declaration on Religious Freedom* in section 5 insists that freedom of choice in education is often the key test in a country or nation as to the sincerity of its commitment to true religious freedom. Monopoly of schools and the exclusion of all religion from education and the educational system in a nation are violations of parental rights.[28]

In the Council's view, therefore, Catholic schools serve much broader purposes than the teaching of religion to a relatively small number of students. Their worth must also be measured in and through their function in the entire human society as well as in the civil order and nation.

Consequently, Catholic parents are reminded of their duty to send their sons and daughters to Catholic schools "wherever and whenever it is possible, of supporting these schools . . . and of cooperating with them in the education of their children" (n. 8).

Archbishop Veuillot of Paris summed up the matter in these words:

"The Council here insists on the traditional discipline of the Church, for the Catholic scholastic institution remains the privileged means of education in the faith. It exists in a special sense in the

---

[28] Cf. *supra*, pp. 74f. In the current controversies on the Catholic schools in the U.S.A., there has been virtually no space given to the concept of these schools as a response to the expressed will and wishes of the parents. Much of the argument misses the point that Catholic parents want Catholic schools.

logic of the faith. Nevertheless, the Declaration is more reserved in its expression than previous canonical texts. . . .

"The qualification 'wherever and whenever it is possible' is important. It is necessary neither to exaggerate nor minimize it. It shows a comprehension by the Church of the actual situation so diverse over the world. It will permit the conferences of bishops to take into account the human, social and economic realities of their respective countries and to give to Catholic parents some appropriate directives."[29]

However, the injunction to parents is not without limitations. Parents are not expected to send their children to Catholic schools without concern for the educational excellence of these schools. Parents have the right of critical discretion in the matter, but of course they have no excuse to neglect the religious education of their children, no matter what school they attend.

Similarly, while the Council proposes newer types of Catholic schools for the poor, the handicapped, adults and the retarded—all in the categories of "special education" (n. 9)—it does not propose an uncontrolled and irresponsible proliferation of second-rate institutions. The point is particularly brought out in reference to colleges and universities:

"This sacred Council . . . earnestly entreats pastors and all the faithful to spare no sacrifice in helping Catholic schools. . . ." (n. 9). "The sacred Synod heartily recommends that Catholic universities and colleges be conveniently located in different parts of the world, but in such a way that

---

[29] Cf. *La Croix*, Nov. 12, 1965.

they are outstanding not for their numbers but for their pursuit of knowledge" (n. 10).

Clearly, then, the Catholic school must indeed be a real "school" in the highest sense of the term. The word "Catholic" as a modifier of the noun "school" must not become a label covering a multitude of mediocrities.

SIGNIFICANT DETAILS IN THE DECLARATION ON CHRISTIAN EDUCATION

As the analysis of the problematic, a review of the history of the text and a study of the major themes have shown, the Council fathers very often desired to have specific injunctions, suggestions and provisions inserted into the text. Consequently, the document is not and indeed could not be a homogeneous or even delicately balanced presentation of thought on education. Like the proverbial camel, it is an animal which looks as though it were put together by a committee; and so it was.

These amendments and suggestions covered a wide range of territory, all the way from sex education to the mention of St. Thomas Aquinas, and they vary in significance and importance. Some are listed herein:

I   *The Church's Right to Educate*

The Council affirmed not only parental rights in education but also the right and duty of the Church to educate, under her supernatural mandate to teach all nations (Prologue) and her mandate in natural law "as a human society capable of educating" (n. 3), and also as responsive to the expressed mandate and desires of parents, including non-Catholics (n. 9).

The text makes its point by reason of its strictures against monopoly of schools which "is opposed to the native rights of the human person. . . ." (n. 6). But an even more direct and more explicit proscription is to be found in the *Declaration on Religious Freedom*. After stating that the parents have the primary right to determine the religious education of their youngsters, the text declares that parents must have true freedom of choice and be "free from unjust burdens either directly or indirectly imposed. . . . Besides, the rights of parents are violated if children are forced to attend classes which stand contrary to the religious convictions of the parents, or if a single system of education is imposed from which religious formation is entirely excluded".[30]

In his intervention in the debate on religious liberty in September, 1965, Cardinal McCann of Capetown, South Africa, strongly affirmed the relationship between freedom in education and religious liberty. The good faith of a State may well be measured, he said, by the practical question of whether or not the Church is free to conduct her schools.

The point of the matter is that in most societies the freedom of schools, freedom of religious instruction and freedom from unjust coercion in education are truly the measure of the sincerity of the State and the effectiveness of its statutes and practices in the matter of religious freedom. If the parents are truly free to choose and the Church is truly free

---

[30] Cf. *supra*, p. 72.

to teach, then the State has passed one important test of religious liberty.[31]

In conclusion, it should be noted here that the Council constantly and consistently assumes, but does not so state, that, given a free choice, parents will indeed most often choose to ask the Church to assist in the education of their youngsters.

II   *The Role of the Teacher*

If the relative merits of the schools of religion of the C.C.D. vis-à-vis the Catholic schools cause some serious questions, this is even more true, *a fortiori*, of the role of the teachers in these areas.

The Declaration does not lack expression of praise, gratitude and esteem for the teacher whose vocation is "beautiful, indeed, and of great importance" (n. 5), for those teachers who care for students in State schools (n. 7), and for those who teach in Catholic schools, upon whom those schools depend "almost entirely". The work of teachers "is, in the real sense of the word, an apostolate" (n. 8). Finally, the entire schema concludes with a plea, particularly to young people, for devotion and self-dedication "to the noble work of education".

There seems to be some confusion in the text inasmuch as it treats of teachers in four different sections, reserving the highest praise for those in Catholic schools. Such, however, was not the intention. Unfortunately, the intervention of Bishop Donohoe, who asked that special notice be taken "of those most devoted laity who are teachers in

---

[31] Cf. *infra*, pp. 110ff., for a treatment of the Church's right to teach.

State-controlled and other schools" and thereby engage in a most wide and true apostolate, was not
included.[32] This idea is found obliquely in the text,
and in the conclusion mention is made of "schools
of every type", but it needs much more emphasis
than is found in the text.

III   *Sex Education*

Two places in the text relate to sex education.
Under the section on Catholic schools (n. 8) the
basic fundament is laid. Teachers are enjoined to
"work as partners with parents and, together with
them in every phase of education, give due consideration to the difference of sex and the proper
ends divine providence assigns to each sex in the
family and in society". Thus, the education of boys
and girls cannot be (nor must the attempt be made
as though it could be) fostered by a denial in practice of their differences, or by a blind ignoring of
the facts. In educational parlance, the provision for
individual differences must begin by a recognition
of the greatest individual difference—that God
created them male and female.

However, as was noted above in the treatment
on the history of the text, the Commission resisted
several attempts to condemn coeducation *per se*.[33]

Perhaps even more striking is the statement
early in the text (n. 1) that children "be given also,
as they advance in years, a positive and prudent
sexual education". This curt text stands in rather

---

[32] Cf. Appendix, p. 156, for text.

[33] Cf. *supra*, p. 32. On Dec. 8, 1957, the Sacred Congregation of Religious issued an instruction on coeducation in
secondary schools which called it "a lesser evil" under certain
circumstances which could be tolerated.

sharp contrast to the four paragraphs on sex education in Pius XI's encyclical *On the Christian Education of Youth*, but it in no way contradicts the encyclical whose strictures on naturalism, "so-called sex education", early exposure to the occasions of sin and denial of original sin in the matter still stand valid. Actually it changes, and indeed develops, only one word of the encyclical—"if":

"If, in this extremely delicate matter, all things considered, some private instruction is found necessary and opportune from those who hold from God the commission to teach and who have the grace of state, every precaution must be taken."

The Council has deleted the one word and in effect is saying that, all things considered today, private instruction *is* necessary and those with the commission to teach and the grace of state should see to a positive and prudent education in the matters of sex. The mood of the imperative has replaced the conditional "if".

IV Colleges and Universities

The intellectual tradition of the Church has maintained that God is truth, that truth is one, and hence that truth can never be found in contradiction to itself. At times, faith in this tradition has wavered and even collapsed in given cases in the long history of the Church; several Council fathers in debate *in aula* in St. Peter's referred pointedly to the celebrated case of Galileo and warned that the Church could not afford other similar cases.

There can be no reason to fear honest and disinterested research; subjects in one field ultimately will not contradict truth in another field, particularly in theology. Sciences stand on their own two feet and are not *per se* subservient even to the sacred sciences; indeed, they furnish material for the latter. Such considerations and ideas as these, expressed in interventions, laid the groundwork for the text.

1. *Scientific Research*

In her own schools the Church "intends that by their very constitution individual subjects be pursued according to their own principles, method and liberty of scientific inquiry" (n. 10). The results will undoubtedly contribute to the harmony between faith and science. The spirit of "the Doctors of the Church and especially of St. Thomas Aquinas" is cited as the model in this quest for the correlation and perhaps even integration of knowledge.

The danger in mentioning St. Thomas lies, of course, in the danger of misinterpreting it to mean that the Church is forever tied to just one philosophy—Aristotelian. As has been cited already, Cardinal Léger had issued just such a warning *in aula* in St. Peter's Basilica. An early draft, going beyond current Canon Law on the matter, especially enjoined theologians and philosophers to treat speculative questions in particular according to the system, teaching and principles of the Angelic Doctor; a later text omitted all mention. The final text calls simply for following "the example" of St. Thomas.[34]

The stress of the text upon research methods extends in a special manner to the sacred sciences "employing up-to-date methods and aids" (n. 11)

---

[34] Another proposal read that "philosophy be treated according to the principles of reason, especially those expounded by St. Thomas. . . ."

and involves solution to that most fundamental of all conciliar questions: the development of dogma.

"Likewise, it is the role of these very faculties to make more penetrating inquiry into the various aspects of the sacred sciences so that an ever-deepening understanding of sacred relevation is obtained . . . and answers are given to questions arising from the development of doctrine" (n. 11).

It is no exaggeration to say that the spirit of Cardinal Newman cast its shadow benevolently over the Council on this most pertinent subject. The Council always had to try to face the question of whether a new development was indeed a true development or a corruption of doctrine and tradition. Newman's criteria with which to judge genuine progress in doctrine—the preservation of type, the continuity of principles, the power of assimilation, the logical sequence, the anticipation of its future and conservation of its past, and finally its chronic vigor—lie beneath the mandate for research in the sacred sciences.[35]

2. *Collaboration and Cooperation*

Perhaps no institutions in the world more jealously and more doggedly guard their autonomy than do universities. The need for utterly disinterested and objective research and inquiry precludes selfish and subjective intervention either by Church or State authorities. Cooperation and collaboration

---

[35] Cf. Cardinal Newman, *Development of Doctrine* (New York: Longmans, Green, 1909), p. 169: "I have maintained that modern Catholicism is nothing else but simply the legitimate growth and complement, that is, the natural and necessary development of the doctrine of the early Church and that its divine authority is included in the diversity of Christianity."

are "the order of the day" (n. 12) but the definition and details are yet another matter not spelled out in the text.

What the relationships to the Holy See, to the Dicastery (Congregation of Seminaries and Universities), to national conferences of bishops and to local ordinaries must be are not included in the text. All attempts to delineate such relationships failed to survive Commission and conciliar objections. However, another document, the *Decree on the Pastoral Office of Bishops in the Church,* contains a clue as to conciliar thinking on the relationship of bishops to schools within a diocese.

In section 35, the text states that all religious, even those exempt, are subject to the authority of local ordinaries in reference to care of souls, worship and the like, and also in what concerns the exercise of the apostolate. "Catholic schools conducted by religious are also subject to the authority of local ordinaries for the purposes of general policy-making and vigilance, but the right of religious to direct them remains intact. Religious are also bound to observe all those things which councils or conferences of bishops shall legitimately prescribe for observance by all."

Although the word "school" has not been defined in the documents, and seems to be applied in section 12 of the education text to "universities" somewhat interchangeably, the universities have, or at least seem to have, both retained their autonomy and widened their mandate for free inquiry and research. Subsequent post-conciliar workings, such as the revision of the Code of Canon Law, the Directorium on Education, and the works of post-conciliar commissions may resolve any doubts as to jurisdiction, competence and authority in reference to colleges and universities.

Study-Club Questions

1. Catholic schools should not become bastions and fortresses of protection against the "outside" world, much less ghettos fostering the growth of pupils as so many hothouse plants sheltered and protected from "the madding crowd's ignoble strife". Explain.

2. What is the relationship between the State and society?

3. Why is monopoly in education, particularly in a pluralistic society, "opposed to the native rights of the human person, to the development and spread of culture and to the peaceful associations of citizens"?

4. A teacher is not simply a legate of the family, or an employee of the State, or a representative of the Church, or an agent for private civic or cultural groups, or the perpetuator of the community culture in the name of the entire society. In many ways, a teacher is and can be all or most of these. Explain.

5. What is the principle of subsidiarity? How does it apply to the relationships between the citizen, the family, and private associations and the government?

6. Briefly discuss the right and duty of the Church to educate under her (a) spiritual mandate, (b) mandate by natural law, (c) mandate through the desire of parents.

7. Sciences stand on their own two feet and are not *per se* subservient to even the sacred sciences; indeed, they furnish material for the latter. Explain.

8. Briefly discuss the conciliar thinking on the relationship of bishops to schools within a diocese, as contained in the *Decree on the Pastoral Office of Bishops in the Church*.

9. What are some of the most important themes and principles in the *Declaration on Christian Education?*

10. What are some of the "surprises" in the Declaration, in view of the original problematic subscribed to by Commission members, the interventions of the Council fathers *in aula* in St. Peter's, and the votes cast pro and con and *juxta modum?*

V

FUTURE DEVELOPMENTS IN LIGHT OF
THE DECLARATION

"Now, obviously, is the time for all good men
to turn in their appraisal of Vatican II—and try
to keep from treading on each other's platitudes. . . .
Each of us has to put all in some sort of perspective,
if only to place himself in the new situation and its
involvements."

These perceptive words of Dr. Albert Outler,
official observer of the World Methodist Council at
Vatican Council II, incisively challenge each Catholic, and school administrators and teachers in particular, to place themselves "in the new situation"
adumbrated by the *Declaration on Christian Education*.

The platitude which bids to become the most
hackneyed is that "the end is the beginning"—that
the fine and noble words committed to paper and
parchment, while of great value *in se*, are only the
platform for action and implementation. Platitudi-
nous or not, Bishop Veuillot, President of the
Episcopal Commission (of France) on the Secular
World, did not hesitate to describe the Declaration
as a stimulus to each Catholic:

"All Catholics will find in the Declaration some
words and some recommendations which concern

them personally: I do not doubt that they will receive them and put them into practice. . . .

"They will be mindful . . . that this text, considered in relationship to and together with the other documents of the Council, opens the way to cooperative action and a renewal for the intellectual and spiritual progress of all men" (*La Croix*, Nov. 12, 1965).

Pope Paul himself, in the public session of Nov. 18, 1965, anticipated the conclusion of Vatican Council II and was quite direct in his call to action:

"This ending is rather a beginning for many projects, the establishment of organizations to collaborate with us in laying down the norms decided by the Council. It is our intention to proceed as soon as possible to establish them. . . ."

One of these "organizations" will be the postconciliar *Declaration on Christian Education* the haps it might be profitable to speculate as to those problems this Commission will attempt to solve. Perhaps it might be equally useful to try to draw some conclusions, some lines of thought for the future, not by some prophetic charism but *out of the text itself*.

What then is the end of the Council and its conciliar *Declaration on Christian Education* the beginning of, the prelude to? What is its thrust, its challenge for the future in the field of education?

The Declaration possesses its own content and matter, but in some ways it cuts across all the other documents of the Council. How, except through Christian education in its broadest sense, will Catholics learn and understand the treasures of the Constitutions, Decrees and Declarations, sixteen in number, which are the fruits of Vatican Council II?

Furthermore, how will those not of the faith so learn? The Declaration, in its spirit and outgoing and outgiving tone as well as in its insistence on education by the Church in all its ramifications as standing at the service of all mankind, challenges every Catholic to capture its spirit and make that spirit incarnate.

What are the future directions of Christian education, then, *in the light of the conciliar text?* Both by reason of what it says and what it does not say, by reason of its positive pronouncements and its omissions and lacunae, certain outlines and adumbrations of the future appear to emerge with some clarity and consistency. These projections may, for convenience, be grouped together under four major categories:

1. There will follow a reappraisal and consequent reassessment of the Church's use of resources in time, talent and money in the field of education.

2. A special reappraisal, analogous to the first, will take place in the field of higher education.

3. Intensive research—historical, legal and philosophical—will be instituted in an attempt to evolve a more viable philosophy of education, particularly in respect to Church-State problems which beset so many countries all over the globe, or, in ordinary parlance, "the school question".

4. The post-conciliar Commission, in addition to composing a *Directorium* (directory of practical conclusions from the conciliar text) and making precise suggestions for the relevant legislation on education in the newly revised Code of Canon Law, will more importantly work toward an updating, an *aggiornamento*, of the great encyclical of Pius XI on education, published in 1929. Perhaps this work

may spark a second *Quadragesimo Anno*, this time in the realm of education, authored and promulgated by Pope Paul VI.

1 *Reapportionment of Resources*

One cannot dispute the charge of Bishop Dammert of Peru that "our organization of our institutions of learning is plainly unequal and indeed partial".[36] The intervention in St. Peter's patently called for the need to reevaluate the uses of resources in Christian education, which in many countries of the world will involve an agonizing reappraisal.

The Council, however, showed no disposition whatever gradually to phase out the Catholic schools of the countries of the world, much less to abandon them to the State. Some bishops, influenced for various reasons—their zeal for national "unity", or their confidence in the schools of religion of the Confraternity of Christian Doctrine and similar programs, or their enthusiasm for ecumenism and the liturgy, or the staggering financial and manpower shortages of their dioceses—would drastically curtail the Church's direct involvement in the foundation and maintenance of schools. Yet these bishops stood in the small minority in 1965, no matter what may be the situation in the year 2000.

The Council solemnly affirmed in its text that both the Catholic school and the religious education of those in other schools are authentic apostolates.

Some observers write and speak as though there were a clear-cut choice and decision between a

---

[36] Cf. *supra*, p. 77.

Catholic school and a State school wherein the religious education of students would be adequately secured. However, the vast majority of bishops who intervened in the Council did not so agree; they feared a State "take-over", and they pointed to such countries as the Sudan and Ceylon and to the Iron Curtain countries, where the "choice" was seemingly to have been respected, but which in point of fact was denied once control was assumed by the State. Governments frequently have declared themselves "competent" in the field of religion, dictating common syllabi and courses of study.[37]

The Catholic Conference of Ontario Bishops (Canada) issued a pastoral letter, September, 1965, in which it met the point directly:

"We are obliged to point out that, even in the practical order, the choice of our province is not between Catholic schools and some form of common, religiously-oriented schools. . . . The only alternative available to us is schools without adequate religious orientation.

"We write this with deep respect for those who have expended and continue to expend great effort in order to obtain some religious orientation for the public schools."

But withal, reapportionment of resources in manpower and materiel challenges national conferences of bishops, religious superiors, bishops and pastors in a diocese. More than ever the challenge is proffered to the layman who holds the answer in his willingness to serve both inside and outside the Catholic school.

There will follow an added emphasis on those organizations devoted to the religious formation of

---

[37] Cf. *supra*, pp. 18f.

students, such as the Newman Apostolate, the Young Christian Students, etc. It is to be hoped that Catholic school facilities will be put at the service of the entire community or parish. The parish will change course from a child-centered, and often a Catholic-school child-centered, parish toward a plan to encompass the youngsters in State schools for religious formation, and adult education as well. Lights may well burn at night and during the vacation periods in the now darkened Catholic schools.[38]

In the United States the Anti-Poverty program, with its Operation Headstart, Job Corps, job retraining, special education for the handicapped, remedial education and other projects of foundations and research institutes, will find a welcome acceptance and warm hospitality not only within the Catholic school facilities but, more importantly, from the faculties thereof—as the conciliar text says, in the service of the entire community.

While the redeployment of talent and personnel will undoubtedly slow down the "proliferation" of Catholic schools, it will have the effect of insuring a better planned growth, consonant with the entire mission of the Church. The reapportionment will inevitably affect the faculties and student bodies, bringing them into closer relationships, *i.e.*, teachers of the Catholic schools and of the C.C.D., Catholic college professors and their Newman counterparts, and especially the pupils and students who, from many reports, have often felt and experienced a

---

38 Cf. Pope Paul, *op. cit.*: "We wish that religious teaching in the schools—while retaining its method, spirit and limits—be considered and coordinated in a unified pastoral framework encompassing family education and training for the liturgical life of the ecclesiastical community."

mutual isolation and segregation in spite of the fact that they are indeed members of "the People of God".

The key lies in the mobilization of that rich and as yet scarcely discovered and tapped resource: the Catholic laity. The net effect will, again hopefully, result in a comprehensive and coherent synthesis of how the Church must meet her responsibilities under her mandate to "teach all nations".

This synthesis will not commend itself to those who advocate the phasing-out of the Catholic school, whether bishops, priests, religious or laymen who sincerely so believe, or to the rugged isolationists and individualists who complacently defend the values of the Catholic school in splendid solitude, oblivious of the research which tends to reveal shortcomings and deficiencies.

Reapportionment is the order of the day in Christian education to meet the needs of the 20th century, a reapportionment evolving into a coherent and balanced synthesis of the Church's resources in time, treasure and talent in education.

II   *The Church in Higher Education*

Holding to the analogue of the position in the fields of elementary and secondary education, the Declaration affirms that the Church must neither abandon her support of Catholic colleges and universities, nor neglect her equally serious obligations toward her sons and daughters in State-supported or other private institutions of higher learning. Again, there must be a reappraisal and reapportionment of resources.

The Council has presented a mandate to Catholic colleges and universities to be and to become schools of excellence, which will act as a true leaven in society by way of the Christian witness for Christ in its graduates, and to accept the challenge of true research in the pursuit of knowledge.

The Challenge to Excellence

"The sacred Synod heartily recommends that Catholic universities and colleges be conveniently located in different parts of the world, but in such a way that they are outstanding not for their numbers but for their pursuit of knowledge" (n. 10).

The pursuit of knowledge, a dynamic concept, is linked in the text to the pursuit of numbers; the Council fathers manifestly disapprove of the search for more and more colleges, universities and students at the expense of excellence and the true pursuit of knowledge. Illogical expansion stands as the enemy of such excellence, and while students can be multiplied with relative ease, competent faculties cannot.

Both a quantitative and qualitative reapportionment lies in the future of Catholic higher educational institutions, a reapportionment and reappraisal that must include, among other things, a collaboration among them and a reemphasis upon the Catholic nature and philosophy of such colleges and universities if they are to be and to become schools of Christian excellence.

Cooperation and collaboration, in the words of the text, are "the order of the day. . . . Since it is altogether necessary in scholastic matters, every means should be employed to foster suitable cooperation among Catholic schools. . . ." (n. 12).

Catholic colleges and universities will, hopefully, continue the movements begun in some countries to merge their efforts in the interests of excellence. The sharing of physical facilities and buildings is a valuable step in this direction; more important, however, is the sharing of faculty. The true measure of excellence rests chiefly, although not exclusively, in the faculty, whether in colleges, universities or seminaries; numbers have ceased to be a valid criterion. But the excellence must be truly Christian.

The reappraisal of those schools which have mimicked their secular counterparts, credit for credit, course for course, "without the pervasive influence of the Catholic mind", will indeed be agonizing. If there be no specific difference, then why and wherefore the Catholic college? The acerbic criticism of the past ten years on the alleged failure of Catholic colleges and universities in the United States to produce Catholic leaders rests as much on the concept "Catholic" as on "leader". Similarly, the emergence of Catholic college graduates in the new nations of Africa into positions of leadership has brought sharp criticism not of their leadership qualities, which they seem to have in abundance, but of their lack of Christian conscience and consciousness.

The law schools of Catholic universities which omit any course in legal ethics, except as found in a State code, neglect the philosophy of law and may well be asked why they do not shut their doors in favor of the State universities. Similarly, those schools of sociology and economics, in which the whole fabric of the social teaching of the Church is given short shrift or is ignored entirely and wherein papal documents are virtually unknown, will, again hopefully, reappraise their curricula and courses of study. Will the great texts of the Church and the Council be seriously studied in the world of today—texts with the deepest thoughts on theology, philosophy, economics, family life, sociology, political theory, and war and peace?

The reevaluation will not point toward turning the Catholic schools (on any level) into moralizing and pietistic institutions or propose a core curriculum built around religious problems. Rather does it suggest an attempt to formulate a logical and balanced and indeed relevant correlation between religion and life, between sacred sciences and other disciplines, in the conviction that religion, if given a false emphasis, either by excess or defect, becomes an intrusion into true education, but if accorded a relevant emphasis, reveals that "between the teachings of faith and every secular subject there exists a relation, which is not special, in the sense that such a relation exists between all branches of knowledge, yet is special because of the paramount importance of religion".[39]

By cooperation and collaboration, then, the Catholic institutions of higher education will take the steps necessary to measure up effectively to the new challenge to graduate men and women who will be truly leaders and at the same time truly Christian. Otherwise, what was once taken as a wry joke, namely, that what many a Catholic college needed was a good Newman Club, may not prove to have been so facetious after all.

The Challenge to Christian Witness

Catholic colleges and universities are also called

39 Cf. F. McGrath, *Newman's University, Idea and Reality* (London: Longmans, Green, 1951), p. 285.

upon to collaborate with all other educational institutions and on all levels, and to be and to become the great leavening influence in society. The entire Church structure and her leadership in the hierarchy and the laity also are given the same injunction: collaboration must extend to the schools of the State, and particularly to all colleges and universities, for herein lies a most urgent and important apostolate.

The Catholic colleges and universities are enjoined by the Council to effect an education that is "a public, enduring and pervasive influence of the Christian mind in the furtherance of culture and [fosters] students . . . molded into men outstanding in their training, ready to undertake weighty responsibilities in society and to witness to the faith in the world" (n. 10).

In all her relevant resources, then, the Catholic Church will markedly extend its witness to Christianity on the secular campus by collaboration between campuses, Catholic and State or private, between faculties and students, and in a special way by a direct apostolate.

"Since the destiny of society and the Church herself is intimately linked with the progress of young people pursuing higher studies, the pastors of the Church are to expend their energies" on students at universities and colleges that are not Catholic and "give abiding spiritual and intellectual assistance. . . ." (n. 10).

There is a clear mandate here for the Newman Apostolate, the Young Christian Students and other similar associations. The text directs bishops' conferences to support such associations and university centers with money and carefully selected and trained personnel.

The Council's directive comes at an opportune time in the United States as major universities are beginning to found and to support schools of religion. The 1927 statement of the State University of Iowa, in its establishment of a school of religion "equal in standing to all other schools and departments on campus", has found many accordant echoes in the past few years:

"Religion theoretically and practically is inseparable from education; hence it should be taught even in tax-supported institutions . . . not indirectly or surreptitiously, but unapologetically, comprehensively, and in line with the best educational practice."[40] The Universities of California, Stanford, Harvard, Yale, Brown and others have moved to include religion as an academic discipline on campus.

Perhaps the prediction easiest to make in this area is that the Church will undoubtedly expand her care for college and university students on secular campuses, using both the Catholic college and university resources in personnel and materiel and also those of the dioceses and parishes.

The Mandate for Research

No section perhaps in all the conciliar documents will be as welcome or welcomed as section 10 which bids colleges and universities to pursue knowledge with true liberty and in the spirit of objective research in all fields, including the sacred sciences which need "a more penetrating inquiry . . . so that an ever-deepening understanding of sacred relevation is obtained. . . ." (n. 11). "Special attention

---

40 Cf. Joseph L. Quinn, *The Catholic World* (Dec. 1965), p. 167.

should be given in Catholic universities and colleges
to institutes that serve primarily the development
of scientific research" (n. 10).

The spirit of this mandate also recognizes the
legitimate autonomy of each subject and discipline
both as to content and to method:

"In those schools dependent on her, [the Church]
intends that by their very constitution individual
subjects be pursued according to their own principles, method and liberty of scientific inquiry . . .
and that, as questions that are new and current are
raised and investigations carefully made according
to the example of the Doctors of the Church and
especially of St. Thomas Aquinas, there may be a
deeper realization of the harmony of faith and
science" (n. 10).

It is interesting to compare Vatican Council I
(Sess. 3, Cap. 4) on this point:

"It is, therefore, far from true that the Church
obstructs the cultivation of human arts and sciences:
the fact is that she assists and furthers them in many
ways. . . . She acknowledges that, just as they come
from God, the Lord of sciences, so, if rightly used,
they lead back to him with the help of his grace.

"Nor does the Church forbid these sciences to
use their own principles and methods in their
respective spheres. This liberty is their right and
she acknowledges it. But she does take every means
to prevent them from opposing God's teaching and
so falling into error, and from overstepping their
own borders, trespassing upon the field of faith, and
so causing confusion therein."[41]

The open spirit and fresh mandate from the
Council will undoubtedly encourage colleges and

---

[41] Cf. F. McGrath, op. cit., p. 286.

universities over the world not only to continue and intensify the pursuit of knowledge, but to become more deeply involved in the affairs of men in the marketplace. The text explicitly points out the object of such research: "questions that are new and current" which call for "investigations carefully made".

The conciliar text, *The Church in the Modern World*, raises many more problems than it could possibly solve: world peace, population, discrimination by reason of race, sex and religion, family life and a score of others. The *Decree on the Pastoral Office of Bishops in the Church* assigns special importance to sociological research, indeed essential for a true measurement and evaluation of Church structures, particularly the parish.[42]

The deep involvement of faculties and students in the political and social questions of these troubled times, hopefully, will turn more to research and deep analysis and synthesis in search of viable solutions.[43] Progress in ecumenism will be

---

[42] There is no implication intended here that "nothing" has been done along these lines. In June, 1965, for example, the sociology department of the University of San Francisco, under the direction of Fr. Eugene Schallert, S.J., published an excellent sociological study of the parishes of San Francisco and thereby furnished both chancery and parish an invaluable tool for future planning.

[43] Perhaps a most significant opportunity might be suggested by way of illustration. Worldwide campaigns in favor of contraception, sterilization and abortion have reached the propaganda stage. There abounds much heat but very little clearly established fact. Japan stands in its second decade of the new syndrome of government promotion of divorce, contraception, sterilization and abortion. The fact remains that there is to date no extensive research to measure just what the effects of this program, admittedly anti-Christian in its ethic, have been. The case calls for research.

the subject of research and evaluation as faculty and student leaders engage in the dialogue enjoined in the text-document on ecumenism. Legal research in countries beset by Church-State issues will help to move the institutions of higher learning further into the mainstream of society.

The Council at once issued the mandate for research and challenged the colleges and universities to face new and current questions and to establish permanent institutes of scientific research.

It is a vote of confidence in Catholic higher education! It is an act of faith in the specifically Catholic intellectual task, namely, to work toward the "unity of truth", truth which cannot contradict itself.

III   *The Philosophy of Christian Education*

The debates and discussions both in Commission and conciliar sessions presage the areas of future development in the field of Christian education. The "divine discontent" with the text has to be interpreted in light of the high expectations of so many bishops and educators around the world and their consequent disappointment, often deeply felt, not so much by reason of what the document says as by what it does not say. As was the case with so many conciliar schemata, the reality never quite measured up to hopes and desires; it was not error or misrepresentation in the text that stimulated opposition, but rather omissions and, according to some, lack of verve, spirit and charismatic flavor in the spirit of *aggiornamento*.[44]

---

[44] 183 voted against the text as a whole on October 14, 1965, the "semi-final ballot"; 38 voted *non placet* in the

A second area of weakness, according to some observers, was an apparent disparity between the strong and incisive interventions, both oral and written, which were presented by the Council fathers, and the relatively mild and attenuated form in which these interventions finally appeared in the schema. Some believed that even the "petite debates" on the text contributed much more than appeared in the final redaction.

These interventions, however, point to the paths of future development and amplification of the document. The text was never intended to stand as an encyclical, treatise or dissertation, much less as an encyclopedia of knowledge on Christian education. The "safety valve" of the text, namely, the post-conciliar Commission, will undoubtedly see to it that the many excellent interventions over the years will not perish, but rather will exert their influence over the future work and developing philosophy of education.

Two major problems, basic and fundamental, etched in large letters, will challenge philosophers of educational theory around the world. The first centers around the title or titles under which the Catholic Church claims the right to educate; the second focuses on the theoretical and practical relationships between society itself and all those agents and agencies with legitimate rights and roles in the field of education.

Both of these important problems, intricate and complex, and only adumbrated in the science of theology and the exegesis of Sacred Scripture and

---

final ballot in the presence of the pope, October 28, 1965. Cf. table in Appendix, p. 145. Several circulars, severely critical, were passed out to the Council fathers in several languages, urging a negative vote.

tradition, must be moved toward viable solutions in a coherent and consistent synthesis if Christian education, in all its ramifications, is to make good sense and indeed be relevant to men in the modern pluralistic State.

The Right of the Church to Educate

"To fulfill the mandate she has received from her divine founder of proclaiming the mystery of salvation to all men and of restoring all things in Christ, Holy Mother the Church must be concerned with the whole of man's life, even the secular part of it insofar as it has a bearing on his heavenly calling. Therefore, she has a role in the progress and development of education" (Prologue).

The rapid transition from the supernatural title to the natural seems desultory, to say the least. Nor does the text redeem itself in n. 3:

"The Church is bound as a mother to give to these children of hers an education by which their whole life can be imbued with the spirit of Christ and, at the same time, to do all she can to promote for all peoples the complete perfection of the human person, the good of earthly society and the building of a world that is more human."

Not surprisingly did Abbé Duclercq, in his memorandum to the Council fathers, complain that the text in this place "is not sufficiently free from a certain confusion. Can it be said that 'the Church as a human society should be recognized as competent to provide for education? Is this directly temporal end really part of the Church's mission?' "

Both passages in the schema closely paraphrased Pope Pius XI's encyclical, *On the Christian Education of Youth* of 1929, wherein the Church's right to educate was described as based upon a "double title in the supernatural order". One rested on the divine mandate to "teach all nations", the other on "the supernatural motherhood of the Church" in the life of grace, the sacraments and doctrine. Several times the titles are qualified by words such as "insofar as religion and morality are concerned" or "insofar as necessary or helpful to Christian education".

The Commission on Education itself had wrestled unsuccessfully with this basic problem and made no pretense that the text offered any solution, even as the encyclical had hesitated to draw clearer lines.[45]

Pope Pius XI wrote that "the education of youth is precisely one of those matters that belong to the Church and to the State 'though in different ways' ".

Precisely what the nature of these "different ways" is remains the challenge to philosophers of education. What are the relationships between supernatural and natural titles? What is provable theologically and also from the natural law? What titles do a "perfect" society, an intermediate association of citizens, an organized school and an educational system responsive to the expressed will of

---

[45] Cf. *supra*, pp. 33f. A proposed statement of the U.S.A. bishops in 1956 treated "The Right of the Church to Teach". It spoke only of the Church's right in the supernatural order to be heard in society and appealed to the concept of the "perfect society": "The right of the Church to teach inheres in her very nature as a perfect society, one whose constitution is altogether independent of any temporal power" (Files of author).

Archbishop Denis Hurley of Durban, South Africa, urged that the Church not use the word "perfect" society because it is open to such misunderstanding. He further stated that the Church as a society is known in the supernatural order and that the problem is to show a bridge to the natural whence the Church has the right, *e.g.*, to teach chemistry or mathematics or other sciences.

the people possess to educate? What does an "indirect right" really mean?

No one questions the right of the Church to educate, even in the so-called secular or profane subjects. However, the future must bring a much needed clarification and indeed an advance over both Pope Pius XI's encyclical and the conciliar text. The Conciliar Commission on Education would seem to be the first to agree and to wish the post-conciliar Commission success in this fundamental area of research.

Society and the State in Education

In spite of all of the attention given to the problems of the relationships of those with both original and derived rights in the field of education, there has not yet emerged a coherent synthesis which has delineated the bounds and limitations as well as the rights and prerogatives of those concerned. For well over a century, and as one major aspect of the Church-State problem, the question of who has rights in education and, as a consequence, how is education to be organized within a given country, nation or State has bemused scholars and political leaders.

The failure to make clear distinctions between "society", a social concept, and the "State", a political concept much narrower in extension, has plagued efforts at evolving a clear philosophical synthesis acceptable to Church, State, family, private associations and the entire community and society itself.

In an inchoate fashion Pope Pius XI distinguished between "the whole society" and "the just rights of the State in regard to the education of its citizens", and between the rights of "civil society" and "civil authority".[46] In his Christian allocutions of 1942 and 1944 Pope Pius XII pleaded for the complete rehabilitation of the juridic order and for the restoration of "the State and its power to the service of human society". The 1944 text in section 37 distinguishes "the person, the State and the government with their respective rights . . . so bound together that they stand or fall together".

Several of the Council fathers made quite clear their conviction that fundamental distinctions were still lacking in Catholic thought on education which stemmed from the failure to assess properly the nature of society itself and the civil society, State or government.

Archbishop Zoa said simply: "It would be better if the distinction between the State and civil society were made more clearly." [47] Bishop Malone was more explicit:

"Consequently, the full schema must include the fundamental distinction between society itself and the State. Society is a social concept which describes the community itself; society means 'the people', or, as we say in English, 'We the People', whereas in contrast the State is a political concept, much narrower in meaning. The State or government is an instrument of society, the political arm of society, and its functions and specific duties must be determined by the consent of the people, *i.e.*, by society itself.[48]

---

[46] Cf. *passim, On the Christian Education of Youth*, 1929.
[47] Cf. *supra*, pp. 47ff.
[48] Compare this statement with that of Pius XII in his Christmas allocution of 1944 on "People and the Masses," "Characteristics Proper to a Democratic Regime" and "State Absolutism" (nn. 17-51, N.C.W.C. edition, 1944).

"Society, then, must be distinguished from the State or government precisely because it is not coterminous with it either in extension or in fundamental rights," the bishop concluded.

While there was some confusion of terms, particularly of the word "State" which in Europe, especially, has been often used as a synonym for "society" and contrasted with government and civil society, yet the underlying concepts were quite clear and clearly grasped. Bishop Malone drew the conclusion:

"Having made this fundamental point, the schema may then proceed to the general principles in education which concern man in the exercise of his highest faculties and in his dignity as a free person.

"The right of a family to equal treatment under the laws of a State or nation; the repudiation of all monopoly in education as an offense against the dignity of a parent to chose the school he wishes for his children; the right of equal justice in relationship to government subsidies in pluralistic societies; the duties of Church and State alike to foster and assist parents in their task and duty— all will be brought into clearer focus." [49]

The theory of State monopoly in education, whether in emerging nations, in the established Occidental countries, in Oriental lands, or under socialistic governments of the East or West, or in "The Third World", has its genesis in the total identification of society and the State, in the belief that the two are in fact coterminous.

---

[49] Cf. Appendix, p. 149, for full text.

Under the consequences of such theory, the State, which properly speaking has no right at all directly to be a teacher or educator, determines what is truly art, truly science, truly culture, and even truly religious or religion.

The post conciliar Commission must reexamine the vexing problem of the *Stato di Diritto* and the *Ordo Juridico* of Pius XII, recognizing the role of the State, which, in view of its purpose, is political, as having the original right and obligation to see to it that its citizens are properly educated to fulfill their duties as members of the body politic as such. The State must indeed enter into the basic question of the body public, namely, how education is to be organized and supported, whether by public or private subsidy or a judicious mixture of both. In fine, the State will be seen as the instrument of society and its scope and competence in the field of education determined by the consent of the people or, better, "society itself".

The conciliar text, as has been pointed out above,[50] makes only one reference to "society as a whole" as distinct from "civil society" (n. 3). Yet such a fact in itself will furnish future researchers with a key to a new vista in the philosophy of education.

Another immediate consequence of this basic premise will be a much more sophisticated and defensible vindication of parental rights to a fair share of public support in their choice of schools.[51] The schema-text very briefly stated the case for the parents in a direct and simple statement of rights "in distributive justice". The conciliar interventions

[50] Cf. *supra,* p. 55.
[51] Cf. *supra,* p. 51.

call for a much more elaborated explanation along the lines suggested by Cardinal Spellman:

"Moreover, if these schools serve the public purpose of popular education, that fact that they may be religious in their orientation should not exclude them from a rightful measure of public support."

The State, as the servant of society, here is being politely told not to intrude into the orientation of the school which, *mutatis mutandis*, is none of its business. Parents are being told to expect support, not in any absolute fashion, but insofar as a public purpose is being served; hence they may have to pay something over and above for what is "extra". They must as their right receive, in both justice and equity, public aid "in due measure".[52]

Finally, the basic distinction of society and the State will help to further research into the proper roles in any society of all those with a legitimate interest and competence in education. If there be defects, for example, in the text's treatment of the role of the State (such accusations have been made), they can logically and intelligently be healed in a fuller treatment by interested scholars, schools of political theory and education, and the post-conciliar Commission.

---

[52] President W. Wayne Dehoney of the Southern Baptist Convention of the U.S.A. "made what may prove to be a prophetic as well as a perceptive statement: 'Absolute separation is imperative where the Church alone is served, but it is not necessarily the best way of dealing with a Church-related college where the public at large is the chief beneficiary'" (*Christian Century*, Dec. 8, 1965). It is curious that so many leaders find such little difficulty in considering colleges a community resource but not elementary or secondary schools. Schools of a bona fide nature belong in the first instance to the community, not to government or Church, and serve the community.

The ecumenical Council shied away from any general treatment of the complexities of Church-State relationships. Step-by-step, modern civilization seems to be working out a new appreciation of the roles of Church and State in society. The Church's *Declaration on Religious Freedom,* with its paragraph on freedom of education, and the *Declaration on Christian Education* are steps in the direction of solutions.

Somewhere in a viable philosophy of education in the modern State and 20th-century society there rests the conviction, inchoate and unclear but nevertheless real, that in a pluralistic society there must be, not of metaphysical necessity but of moral necessity, a pluralistic answer. Neither the totalitarian State's solution of rigid uniformity, nor even, in some countries, the democratic State's solution of the will of the majority *alone*, secures the true freedom of education.

IV *A New Encyclical on Education*

All through the pre-conciliar and conciliar stages, the members of the Commission on Education were aware, indeed acutely aware, of the relationship of their work to the encyclical *On the Christian Education of Youth* of 1929. The desire not simply to restate what the encyclical had already said so well, but also to advance from the thought of the encyclical in the spirit of Vatican Council II guided the making of the text. After the document text was made public many educators and some bishops renewed their pleas that the Church needed another encyclical on education to do what the Council could not.

The post-conciliar Commission, voted into existence *in aula* in St. Peter's, has a mandate from the Church itself to proceed to face with deliberate speed the great difficulties inherent in the attempt to express anything of validity in education which would apply meaningfully to the various nations on earth. Under the conciliar process, with its myriad of limitations, it was scarcely possible to meet the task as scholars and researchers would and could. Perhaps the new Commission will lay the foundations for a new encyclical on education.

Be that as it may, the post-conciliar Commission must, if precedents are to be followed, compile the new *Directorium* or compendium of educational matters, which, though of value, were not sufficiently important to be included in the brief text. Much like the famous *Catechism* of Trent, the *Directorium* will exhibit in more detail the "mind of the Council fathers". A second project facing the Commission will be its contribution to the revision of the Code of Canon Law, including those changes suggested by the members of all the sub-committees and implied from the words of the conciliar text itself.[53]

But any study following closely upon the Council, whether it leads to a new encyclical or not, will have to take up, at the very least, some of the subjects which were barely mentioned or omitted entirely.

Two major questions have already been treated

---

[53] The Plenary Commission appointed a sub-commission under the chairmanship of Archbishop John Cody of Chicago to care for the suggested changes in the Code of Canon Law in the field of education, including seminaries. One item, *e.g.*, was the proposal to grant the Diocesan Superintendent of Schools canonical status.

at some length, namely, the clarification of the bases upon which the Catholic Church claims the right to teach, and the fundamental distinction between society as such and its political arm, the State.[54] No true progress can even be attempted without attention to these two major problems. However, two more concern the pupil and the teacher.

The Pupil

The Declaration did affirm the right of each youngster to an adequate education, but it gave very little attention to the pupil as such. While emphasizing parental rights over children, which Pope Pius XI took pains to say were not "absolute and despotic", the text did not describe the educand in terms of his own legitimate rights in the choice of his education, in the selection of his own vocation in life and in the God-given autonomy in balanced harmony with other valid interests, whether Church, State, family or society itself.[55]

Bishop Elchinger made the point directly in his intervention: "No one is the possessor of infants or youths: neither the State, nor society, nor the Church, nor even the parents themselves. All must serve them, each one according to his own office. So the State, even though it has its own schools, acts unjustly if it imposes on its schools its own ideology which the State cannot hold since it must serve uniquely the common good of society, *i.e.,*

---

[54] Cf. *supra*, pp. 70ff.

[55] Cf. *Christian Education of Youth* (Glen Rock: Paulist Press, 1944), p. 46. Again this idea, which was included in early texts, "got lost" in the conciliar process.

the community. The spirit of the Gospel condemns all totalitarianism." [56]

The text's one line on the necessity of suitable sex education should be an excellent starting point for a full treatment of a most important, yet delicate subject. Not unrelated is the matter of education for vocation in life, whether for the married, the single, the religious or the priest. In the same vein, the relationship to the State, especially with reference to civic education in the school and in Christian education, calls for amplification and development. The State and its proper role in education have all too often been minimized in Catholic literature. The word "subsidiarity" has been commonly employed as a weapon to keep the State out of education as though its *only* role was supplementary and secondary.

Greater attention to the pupil himself, as a child of God, as a complete human person in his age, and in his own human nature will undoubtedly help to balance any further statements on Christian education.

The Teacher

While the teacher receives a meed of deserved praise in the conciliar text, and although young people are urged to become teachers in a most worthy apostolate, the Declaration could not enter into details sufficiently.

Although the notion of "apostolate" is inferentially extended to all teachers, it is all but lost in reference to teachers in State schools. The praise of teachers seems to confine itself to those teaching under Church auspices, rather than to all teachers;

---

[56] Cf. *supra*, footnote 20, p. 69.

he latter in fact was the intention of the sub-commission on schools in the Conciliar Commission.[57]

A new look at the teacher will see him as an
essential factor in the Christian presence in the
entire world of education and schools, as a servant,
and as a Christian servant—not in a narrow sectarian sense—who loves all his students and truly
represents all those with a legitimate role in education. The teacher will be delineated in his profession as: the delegate of the parent; a witness of the
Christian message, *mutatis mutandis* in some countries; civil servant; representative of various intermediate groups and societies; and the representative
of society itself in the handing down of the cultural
heritage of the community. All of these adumbrations are to be found in the Declaration; the ex-
panding of them in detail will be of the greatest
importance for the future.[58]

Will there be a new encyclical as a result of the
work of the post-conciliar Commission on Education, an encyclical which would bring up-to-date

---

[57] Cf. Bishop Donohoe in the Appendix, p. 156. Pope Paul
VI said on Aug. 28, 1964: "We ... send our greeting and bless-
ing to all the good public and private schools, to all who promote and direct them, to those who therein exercise the delicate and sublime mission of educators and teachers. . . ."
(*The Pastoral Ministry of Secondary Schools*, N.C.W.C.,
Sept. 22, 1964) .

[58] The implications for teachers' training institutes seem
evident. It might be remarked in passing that the Commission felt it much more important to underscore the need
for good teachers than to bemoan philosophical and ideological errors in and about the world of education.

Speaking with Cardinal Colombo, a member of the Conciliar Commission on Education, Pope Paul VI said that he
was satisfied with the text of the *Declaration on Christian
Education* and that "the vocation of the teacher is a privileged form of the apostolate of the Church". Cf. Hoffer,
op. cit., p. 1041.

On the Christian Education of Youth? The prospect seems not only feasible but very desirable, and it will call for the cooperation and contributions of many, especially of experts in all the fields of education around the world.

The *Declaration on Christian Education* of Vatican Council II stands as an invitation to research and further progress in harmony with the other great documents of this great Council.

Study-Club Questions

1. Reapportionment is the order of the day in Christian education to meet the needs of the 20th century. What kind of reapportionment is necessary?

2. How can the Catholic Church markedly extend her witness to Christianity on the secular campus?

3. Why is religion, theoretically and practically, inseparable from education?

4. What suggestions would you make to move Catholic institutions of higher learning further into the mainstream of society?

5. Schools of a bona fide nature belong in the first instance to the community, not to the government or the Church, and they serve the community. Discuss.

6. What qualifications are necessary to become a good teacher?

7. In light of the Declaration, what are the future directions of Christian education?

8. Is the State competent in the field of religion to dictate common syllabi and courses of religion?

9. In a pluralistic society there must be, not of metaphysical necessity but of moral necessity, a pluralistic answer to the problem of education. Explain.

10. Mention two important subjects in the field of education which were barely mentioned or omitted entirely in the *Declaration on Christian Education*.

De Educatione Christiana

THE DECLARATION

ON

CHRISTIAN EDUCATION

OF

VATICAN COUNCIL II

Promulgated by Pope Paul VI
October 28, 1965

PAUL BISHOP

THE DECLARATION
ON
CHRISTIAN EDUCATION

PROLOGUE

THE SACRED ECUMENICAL COUNCIL has considered with care how extremely important education is in the life of man and how its influence ever grows in the social progress of this age.[1]

---

[1] Among many documents illustrating the importance of education, cf. especially Benedict XV, Apostolic Letter *Communes litteras*, April 10, 1919: *A.A.S.* 11 (1919), p. 172; Pius XI, Encyclical Letter *Divini Illius Magistri*, Dec. 31, 1929: *A.A.S.* 22 (1930), pp. 49-86; Pius XII, Allocution *To the Youths of Italian Catholic Action*, April 20, 1946: *Discourses and Radio Messages of His Holiness Pius XII*, 8, pp. 53-7; Pius XII, Allocution *To Fathers of French Families*, Sept. 18, 1951: *Discourses and Radio Messages of His Holiness Pius XII*, 13, pp. 241-5; John XXIII, 30th-Anniversary Message on the Publication of the Encyclical Letter *Divini Illius Magistri*, Dec. 30, 1959: *A.A.S.* 52 (1960), pp. 57-9; Paul VI, Allocution *To Members of Federated Institutes Dependent on Ecclesiastical Authority*, Dec. 30, 1963: *Encyclicals and Dis-*

Indeed, the circumstances of our time have made it easier and at the same time more urgent to educate young people and, what is more, to continue the education of adults. Men are more aware of their own dignity and position; more and more they want to take an active part in social and especially in economic and political life.[2] Enjoying more leisure, as they sometimes do, men find that the remarkable development of technology and scientific investigation and the new means of communication offer them an opportunity of attaining more easily their cultural and spiritual inheritance and of fulfilling one another in the closer ties between groups and even between peoples.

Consequently, attempts are being made everywhere to promote more education. The rights of men to an education, particularly the primary rights of children and parents, are being proclaimed and recognized in public documents.[3] As the number of pupils rapidly increases, schools are multiplied and expanded far and wide and other educational institutions are established. New experi-

---

courses of His Holiness Paul VI (Rome, 1964), pp. 601-3. Above all are to be consulted the *Acts and Documents of Vatican Council II* appearing in the first series of the antepreparatory phase, 3, pp. 363-4, 370-1, 373-4.

[2] Cf. John XXIII, Encyclical Letter *Mater et Magistra*, May 15, 1961: *A.A.S.* 53 (1961), pp. 413, 415-7, 424; John XXIII, Encyclical Letter *Pacem in terris*, April 11, 1963: *A.A.S.* 55 (1963), pp. 278f.

[3] Cf. the *Declaration on the Rights of Man*, Dec. 10, 1948, adopted by the General Assembly of the United Nations; cf. also the *Declaration on the Rights of Children*, Nov. 20, 1959; cf. additional protocol to the Convention Safeguarding the Rights of Men and Fundamental Liberties, Paris, March 20, 1952; in regard to that universal profession of the character of human laws, cf. John XXIII, Encyclical Letter *Pacem in terris*, April 11, 1963: *A.A.S.* 55 (1963), pp. 295f.

ments are conducted in methods of education and teaching. Great attempts are being made to obtain education for all, even though vast numbers of children and young people are still deprived of even rudimentary training and so many others lack a suitable education in which truth and love are developed together.

To fulfill the mandate she has received from her divine founder of proclaiming the mystery of salvation to all men and of restoring all things in Christ, Holy Mother the Church must be concerned with the whole of man's life, even the secular part of it insofar as it has a bearing on his heavenly calling.[4] Therefore, she has a role in the progress and development of education. Hence this sacred Synod declares certain fundamental principles of Christian education, especially in schools. These principles will have to be developed at greater length by a special post-conciliar Commission and applied by episcopal conferences to varying local situations.

1. All men of every race, condition and age, since they enjoy the dignity of a human being, have an inalienable right to an education[5] that is in keeping with their ultimate goal,[6] their ability, their sex and the culture and tradition of their country, and also in harmony with their fraternal association

----

[4] Cf. John XXIII, Encyclical Letter *Mater et Magistra*, May 15, 1961: *A.A.S.* 53 (1961), p. 402; Vatican Council II, *Dogmatic Constitution on the Church*, n. 17: *A.A.S.* 57 (1965), p. 21.

[5] Cf. Pius XII, Radio Message of Dec. 24, 1942: *A.A.S.* 35 (1943), pp. 12, 19; John XXIII, Encyclical Letter *Pacem in terris*, April 11, 1963: *A.A.S.* 55 (1963), pp. 259f.; also cf. declarations cited on the rights of man in footnote 3.

[6] Cf. Pius XI, Encyclical Letter *Divini Illius Magistri*, Dec. 31, 1929: *A.A.S.* 22 (1930), pp. 50f.

with other peoples in the fostering of true unity and peace on earth. For a true education aims at the formation of the human person in the pursuit of his ultimate end and of the good of the societies of which, as man, he is a member, and in whose obligations, as an adult, he will share.

Therefore, children and young people must be helped, with the aid of the latest advances in psychology and the arts and science of teaching, to develop harmoniously their physical, moral and intellectual endowments so that they may gradually acquire a mature sense of responsibility in striving endlessly to form their own lives properly and in pursuing true freedom as they surmount the vicissitudes of life with courage and constancy. Let them be given also, as they advance in years, a positive and prudent sexual education. Moreover, they should be trained to take their part in social life so that, properly instructed in the necessary and opportune skills, they can become actively involved in various community organizations, open to discourse with others and willing to do their best to promote the common good.

This sacred Synod likewise declares that children and young people have a right to be motivated to appraise moral values with a right conscience and to embrace them with a personal adherence, together with a deeper knowledge and love of God. Consequently, it earnestly entreats all those who hold a position of public authority or who are in charge of education to see to it that youth is never deprived of this sacred right. It further exhorts the sons of the Church to give their attention with generosity to the entire field of education, having especially in mind the need of extending very soon the benefits of a suitable education and training to everyone in all parts of the world.[7]

2. Since all Christians have become by rebirth of water and the Holy Spirit a new creature[8] so that they should be called and should be children of God, they have a right to a Christian education. A Christian education does not merely strive for the maturing of a human person as just now described, but has as its principal purpose this goal: that the baptized, while they are gradually introduced to the knowledge of the mystery of salvation, become ever more aware of the gift of faith they have received, and that they learn in addition how to worship God the Father in spirit and truth (cf. John 4, 23), especially in liturgical action, and be conformed in their personal lives according to the new man created in justice and holiness of truth (Eph. 4, 22-24); also, that they develop into perfect manhood, to the mature measure of the fullness of Christ (cf. Eph. 4, 13) and strive for the growth of the mystical body; moreover that, aware of their calling, they learn not only how to bear witness to the hope that is in them (cf. 1 Pet. 3, 15) but also how to help in the Christian formation of the world that takes place when natural powers, viewed in the full consideration of man redeemed by Christ, contribute to the good of the whole of society.[9] Therefore, this sacred Synod recalls to pastors of souls their most

---

[7] Cf. John XXIII, Encyclical Letter *Mater et Magistra*, May 15, 1961: *A.A.S.* 53 (1961), pp. 441f.

[8] Cf. Pius XI, Encyclical Letter *Divini Illius Magistri*, *loc. cit.*, p. 83.

[9] Cf. Vatican Council II, *Dogmatic Constitution on the Church*, n. 36: *A.A.S.* 57 (1965), pp. 41f.

serious obligation to see to it that all the faithful, but especially the youth who are the hope of the Church, enjoy this Christian education.[10]

3. Since parents have brought children to life, they are bound by the most serious obligation to educate their offspring and therefore must be recognized as the primary and principal educators.[11] This role in education is so important that only with difficulty can it be supplied where it is lacking. Parents are the ones who must create a family atmosphere animated by love and respect for God and man, in which the well-rounded personal and social education of children is fostered. Hence, the family is the first school of the social virtues that every society needs. It is particularly in the Christian family, enriched by the grace and office of the sacrament of matrimony, that children should be taught from their early years to have a knowledge of God according to the faith received in baptism, to worship him and to love their neighbor. Here too they find their first experience of a wholesome human society and of the Church. Finally, it is through the family that they are gradually led to a companionship with their fellowmen and with the People of God. Let parents, then, recognize the inestimable importance a truly Christian family has for the life and progress of God's own people.[12]

---

[10] Cf. Vatican Council II, *Decree on the Pastoral Office of Bishops in the Church*, nn. 12-14.

[11] Cf. Pius XI, Encyclical Letter *Divini Illius Magistri*, *loc. cit.*, pp. 59f.; Pius XI, Encyclical Letter *Mit brennender Sorge*, March 14, 1937: *A.A.S.* 29 (1937), pp. 164f.; Pius XII, Allocution *To the First National Congress of the Italian Catholic Teachers' Association (A.I.M.C.)*, Sept. 8, 1946: *Discourses and Radio Messages of His Holiness Pius XII*, 8, p. 218.

[12] Cf. Vatican Council II, *Dogmatic Constitution on the Church*, nn. 11, 35: *A.A.S.* 57 (1965), pp. 16, 40f.

The family which has the primary duty of imparting education needs the help of society as a whole. In addition, therefore, to the rights of parents and others to whom the parents entrust a share in the work of education, certain rights and duties belong indeed to *civil society* whose role is to direct what is required for the common temporal good. Its function is to promote the education of youth in many ways, namely: to protect the duties and rights of parents and others who share in education, and to give them aid; according to the principle of subsidiarity, when the endeavors of parents and other societies are lacking, to carry out the work of education in accordance with the wishes of the parents; and, moreover, as the common good demands, to build schools and institutions.[13]

Finally, in a special way, the duty of educating belongs to the Church, not merely because she must be recognized as a human society capable of educating, but especially because she has the responsibility of announcing the way of salvation to all men, of communicating the life of Christ to those who believe, and, in her unfailing solicitude, of assisting men to be able to come to the fullness of this life.[14] The Church is bound as a mother to give to these

[13] Cf. Pius XI, Encyclical Letter *Divini Illius Magistri*, *loc. cit.*, pp. 63f.; Pius XII, Radio Message of June 1, 1941: *A.A.S.* 33 (1941), p. 200; Pius XII, Allocution *To the First National Congress of the Italian Catholic Teachers' Association*, Sept. 8, 1946: *Discourses and Radio Messages of His Holiness Pius XII*, 8, p. 218; in regard to the principle of subsidiarity, cf. John XXIII, Encyclical Letter *Pacem in terris*, April 11, 1963: *A.A.S.* 55 (1963), p. 294.

[14] Cf. Pius XI, Encyclical Letter *Divini Illius Magistri*, *loc. cit.*, pp. 53f., 56f.; Pius XI, Encyclical Letter *Non abbiamo bisogno*, June 29, 1931: *A.A.S.* 23 (1931), pp. 311f.; Pius XII, *Letter from the Secretary of State to the 28th Italian Social Week*, Sept. 20, 1955: *L'Osservatore Romano*, Sept. 29, 1955.

children of hers an education by which their whole life can be imbued with the spirit of Christ and, at the same time, to do all she can to promote for all peoples the complete perfection of the human person, the good of earthly society and the building of a world that is more human.[15]

4. In fulfilling her educational role, the Church, eager to employ all suitable aids, is concerned especially about those which are her very own. Foremost among these is catechetical instruction[16] which enlightens and strengthens the faith, nourishes life according to the spirit of Christ, leads to intelligent and active participation in the liturgical mystery[17] and gives motivation for apostolic activity. The Church esteems highly and seeks to penetrate and ennoble with her own spirit other aids also which belong to the general heritage of man and which are of great influence in forming souls and molding men, such as the media of communication,[18] various groups for mental and physical development, youth associations and, in particular, schools.

5. Among all educational instruments the school

---

[15] The Church praises those local, national, and international civil authorities who, conscious of the urgent necessity in these times, expend all their energy so that all peoples may benefit from more education and human culture. Cf. Paul VI, Allocution *To the General Assembly of the United Nations,* Oct. 4, 1965: *L'Osservatore Romano,* Oct. 6, 1965.

[16] Cf. Pius XI, Motu Proprio *Orbem Catholicum,* June 29, 1923: *A.A.S.* 15 (1923), pp. 327-9; Pius XI, Decree *Provide sane,* Jan. 12, 1935: *A.A.S.* 27 (1935), pp. 145-52; cf. also Vatican Council II, *Decree on the Pastoral Office of Bishops in the Church,* nn. 13-14.

[17] Cf. Vatican Council II, *Constitution on the Sacred Liturgy,* n. 14: *A.A.S.* 56 (1964), p. 104.

[18] Cf. Vatican Council II, *Decree on the Media of Social Communications,* nn. 13-14: *A.A.S.* 56 (1964), pp. 149f.

has a special importance.[19] It is designed not only to develop with special care the intellectual faculties but also to form the ability to judge rightly, to hand on the cultural legacy of previous generations, to foster a sense of values and to prepare for professional life. Among pupils of different talents and backgrounds it promotes friendly relations and fosters a spirit of mutual understanding, and it establishes, as it were, a center whose work and progress must be shared together by families, teachers, and associations of various types that foster cultural, civic and religious life, as well as by civil society and the entire human community.

Beautiful, indeed, and of great importance is the vocation of all those who aid parents in fulfilling their duties and who, as representatives of the human community, undertake the task of education in schools. This vocation demands special qualities of mind and heart, very careful preparation and continuing readiness to renew and to adapt.

6. Parents who have the primary and inalienable right and duty to educate their children must enjoy true liberty in their choice of schools. Consequently, the government which has the obligation to protect and defend the rights of citizens must see to it, in its concern for distributive justice, that public assistance is given in such a way that parents are truly free to choose according to their conscience the schools they want for their children.[20]

---

[19] Cf. Pius XI, Encyclical Letter *Divini Illius Magistri, loc. cit.*, p. 76; Pius XII, Allocution *To the Bavarian Association of Catholic Teachers*, Dec. 31, 1956: *Discourses and Radio Messages of His Holiness Pius XII*, 18, p. 746.

[20] Cf. Provincial Council of Cincinnati III, a. 1861: *Collatio Laecensis*, 3, col. 1240, c/d; Pius XI, Encyclical Letter *Divini Illius Magistri, loc. cit.*, pp. 60, 63f.

In addition, it is the task of the State to see to it that all citizens are able to come to a suitable share in culture and are properly prepared to exercise their civic duties and rights. Therefore, the State must protect the right of children to an adequate school education, check on the ability of teachers and the excellence of their training, look after the health of the pupils and, in general, promote the entire work of the schools. But it must always keep in mind the principle of subsidiarity so that there is no kind of school monopoly, for this is opposed to the native rights of the human person, to the development and spread of culture, to the peaceful association of citizens and to the pluralism that exists today in ever so many societies.[21]

Therefore, this sacred Synod exhorts the faithful to assist to their utmost in finding suitable methods of education and programs of study and in forming teachers who can give youth a true education. Through the associations of parents in particular, they should further with their assistance all the work of the school, but especially the moral education it must impart.[22]

7. Feeling very keenly the weighty responsibility

---

[21] Cf. Pius XI, Encyclical Letter *Divini Illius Magistri*, *loc. cit.*, p. 63; Pius XI, Encyclical Letter *Non abbiamo bisogno*, June 29, 1931: *A.A.S.* 23 (1931), p. 305; Pius XII, *Letter from the Secretary of State to the 28th Italian Social Week*, Sept. 20, 1955: *L'Osservatore Romano*, Sept. 29, 1955; Paul VI, Allocution *To The Association of Italian Christian Workers (A.C.L.I.)*, Oct. 6, 1963: *Encyclicals and Discourses of His Holiness Paul VI*, 1 (Rome, 1964), p. 230.

[22] Cf. John XXIII, 30th-Anniversary Message on the Publication of the Encyclical Letter *Divini Illius Magistri*, Dec. 30, 1959: *A.A.S.* 52 (1960), p. 57.

of diligently caring for the moral and religious education of all her children, the Church must be present with her own special affection and help for the great number who are being trained in schools that are other than Catholic. This is possible by the witness of the lives of those who teach and direct them, by the apostolic action of their fellow-students,[23] but especially by the ministry of priests and laymen who give them the doctrine of salvation in a way suited to their age and circumstances and provide spiritual aid in every way the times and conditions allow.

The Church reminds parents of the duty that is theirs to arrange and even demand that their children be able to enjoy these aids and advance in their Christian formation to a degree that is abreast of their development in secular subjects. Therefore, the Church esteems highly those civil authorities and societies which, bearing in mind the pluralism of contemporary society and respecting religious freedom, assist families so that the education of their children can be imparted in all schools according to the individual moral and religious principles of the families.[24]

8. The influence of the Church in the field of education is shown in a special manner by the Catholic school. No less than other schools does the Catholic school pursue cultural goals and the human formation of youth. But its proper function is

---

[23] The Church also considers it as an apostolic action of great worth when Catholic teachers and associates work in these schools.

[24] Cf. Pius XII, Allocution *To the Bavarian Association of Catholic Teachers*, Dec. 31, 1956: *Discourses and Radio Messages of His Holiness Pius XII*, 18, pp. 745f.

to create for the school community a special atmosphere animated by the Gospel spirit of freedom and charity, to help youth grow according to the new creatures they were made through baptism as they develop their own personalities, and finally to order the whole of human culture to the news of salvation so that the knowledge the students gradually acquire of the world, life and man is illumined by faith.[25] So, indeed, the Catholic school, while it is open, as it must be, to the conditions of the contemporary world, leads its students to promote efficaciously the good of the earthly city and also prepares them for service in the spread of the kingdom of God, so that by leading an exemplary apostolic life they become, as it were, a saving leaven in the human community.

Since, therefore, the Catholic school can be such an aid to the fulfillment of the mission of the People of God and to the fostering of the dialogue between the Church and mankind to the benefit of both, it retains, even in our present circumstances, the utmost importance. Consequently, this sacred Synod proclaims anew what has already been taught in several documents of the magisterium,[26] namely, the right of the Church freely to establish and to

---

[25] Cf. Provincial Council of Westminster I, a. 1852: *Collatio Laecensis*, 3, col. 1334, a/b; Pius XI, Encyclical Letter *Divini Illius Magistri, loc. cit.*, pp. 77f.; Pius XII, Allocution *To the Bavarian Association of Catholic Teachers*, Dec. 31, 1956: *Discourses and Radio Messages of His Holiness Pius XII*, 18, p. 746; Paul VI, Allocution *To the Members of Federated Institutes Dependent on Ecclesiastical Authority (F.I.D.A.E.)*, Dec. 30, 1963: *Encyclicals and Discourses of His Holiness Paul VI*, 1 (Rome, 1964), pp. 602f.

[26] Cf. especially the documents mentioned in footnote 1. Moreover, this right of the Church has been proclaimed by many provincial conferences as well as in the most recent declarations of very many episcopal conferences.

conduct schools of every type and level. And the Council calls to mind that the exercise of a right of this kind contributes in the highest degree to the protection of freedom of conscience and the rights of parents, as well as to the betterment of culture itself.

But let teachers recognize that the Catholic school depends upon them almost entirely for the accomplishment of its goals and programs.[27] They should therefore be very carefully prepared so that both in secular and religious knowledge they are equipped with suitable qualifications and also with a pedagogical skill that is in keeping with the findings of the contemporary world. Intimately linked in charity to one another and to their students and endowed with an apostolic spirit, may teachers by their life as much as by their instruction bear witness to Christ, the unique teacher. Let them work as partners with parents and, together with them in every phase of education, give due consideration to the difference of sex and the proper ends divine providence assigns to each sex in the family and in society. Let them do all they can to stimulate their students to act for themselves and even after graduation continue to assist them with advice, friendship and by establishing special associations imbued with the true spirit of the Church. The work of these teachers, this sacred Synod declares, is, in the real sense of the word, an apostolate most suited to and necessary for our times

---

[27] Cf. Pius XI, Encyclical Letter *Divini Illius Magistri, loc. cit.*, pp. 80f; Pius XII, Allocution *To the Catholic Association of Italian Teachers in Secondary Schools (U.C.I.I.M.),* Jan. 5, 1954: *Discourses and Radio Messages of His Holiness Pius XII*, 15, pp. 551-6; John XXIII, Allocution *To the 6th Congress of the Association of Catholic Italian Teachers,* Sept. 5, 1959: *Discourses, Messages, Conversations of His Holiness John XXIII*, 1 (Rome, 1960), pp. 427-31.

and at the same time a true service offered to society. The Council also reminds Catholic parents of the duty of entrusting their children to Catholic schools wherever and whenever it is possible, of supporting these schools to the best of their ability and of cooperating with them in the education of their children.[28]

9. To this concept of a Catholic school all schools that are in any way dependent on the Church must conform as far as possible, although the Catholic school is to take on different forms in keeping with local circumstances.[29] Thus the Church considers very dear to her heart those Catholic schools, found especially in the areas of the new churches, which are also attended by students who are not Catholics.

Attention should be paid to the needs of today in establishing and directing Catholic schools. Therefore, though primary and secondary schools, the foundation of education, must still be fostered, great importance is to be attached to those which are required in a particular way by contemporary conditions such as professional[30] and technical schools, centers for educating adults and promoting social welfare or for the retarded in need of special care, and also schools for preparing teachers for religious instruction and other types of education.

---

[28] Cf. Pius XII, Allocution *To the Catholic Association of Italian Teachers in Secondary Schools, loc. cit.*, p. 555.

[29] Cf. Paul VI, Allocution *To the International Office of Catholic Education (O.I.E.C.)*, Feb. 25, 1964: *Encyclicals and Discourses of His Holiness Paul VI*, 2 (Rome, 1964), p. 232.

[30] Cf. Paul VI, Allocution *To the Christian Association of Italian Workers*, Oct. 6, 1963: *Encyclicals and Discourses of His Holiness Paul VI*, 1 (Rome, 1964), p. 229.

This sacred Council of the Church earnestly entreats pastors and all the faithful to spare no sacrifice in helping Catholic schools fulfill their function in a continually more perfect way, and especially in caring for the needs of those who are poor in the goods of this world or who are deprived of the assistance and affection of a family or who are strangers to the gift of faith.

10. The Church is also concerned with schools of a higher level, especially universities and colleges. In those schools dependent on her, she intends that by their very constitution individual subjects be pursued according to their own principles, method and liberty of scientific inquiry in such a way that an ever deeper understanding in these fields will be obtained and that, as questions that are new and current are raised and investigations carefully made according to the example of the Doctors of the Church and especially of St. Thomas Aquinas, there may be a deeper realization of the harmony of faith and science.[31] Thus there is accomplished a public, enduring and pervasive influence of the Christian mind in the furtherance of culture, and the students of these institutions are molded into men truly outstanding in their training, ready to undertake weighty responsibilities in society and to witness to the faith in the world.[32]

---

[31] Cf. Paul VI, Allocution *To the International Thomistic Congress*, Sept. 10, 1965: *L'Osservatore Romano*, Sept. 13-14, 1965.

[32] Cf. Pius XII, Allocution *To Teachers and Students of French Institutes of Higher Catholic Education*, Sept. 21, 1950: *Discourses and Radio Messages of His Holiness Pius XII*, 12, pp. 219-21; Pius XII, *Letters to the 22nd Congress of Pax Romana*, Aug. 12, 1952: *Discourses and Radio Messages of His Holiness Pius XII*, 14, pp. 567-9; John XXIII,

In Catholic universities where there is no faculty of sacred theology, there should be established an institute or chair of sacred theology in which there should be lectures suited to lay students. Since science advances by means of the investigations peculiar to higher scientific studies, special attention should be given in Catholic universities and colleges to institutes that serve primarily the development of scientific research.

The sacred Synod heartily recommends that Catholic universities and colleges be conveniently located in different parts of the world, but in such a way that they are outstanding not for their numbers but for their pursuit of knowledge. Matriculation should be readily available to students of real promise, even though they be of slender means, and especially to students from the newly emerging nations.

Since the destiny of society and of the Church herself is intimately linked with the progress of young people pursuing higher studies,[33] the pastors of the Church are not only to expend their energies on the spiritual life of students who attend Catholic universities, but, solicitous for the spiritual formation of all their children, they must see to it, after consultations among bishops, that even at universities that are not Catholic there should be associa-

---

Allocution *To the Federation of Catholic Universities*, April 1, 1959: *Discourses, Messages, Conversations of His Holiness John XXIII*, 1 (Rome, 1960), pp. 226-9; Paul VI, Allocution *To the Academic Senate of the Catholic University of Milan*, April 5, 1964: *Encyclicals and Discourses of His Holiness Paul VI*, 2 (Rome, 1964), pp. 438-43.

[33] Cf. Pius XII, Allocution *To the Academic Senate and Students of the University of Rome*, June 15, 1952: *Discourses and Radio Messages of His Holiness Pius XII*, 14, p. 208: "The direction of today's society is principally placed in the mentality and hearts of the universities of today."

tions and university centers under Catholic auspices in which priests, religious and laity, carefully selected and prepared, should give abiding spiritual and intellectual assistance to the youth of the university. Whether in Catholic universities or others, young people of greater ability who seem suited for teaching or research should be especially helped and encouraged to undertake a teaching career.

11. The Church expects much from the zealous endeavors of the faculties of the sacred sciences,[34] for to them she entrusts the very serious responsibility of preparing her own students not only for the priestly ministry, but especially for teaching in the seats of higher ecclesiastical studies or for promoting learning on their own or for undertaking the work of a more rigorous intellectual apostolate. Likewise, it is the role of these very faculties to make more penetrating inquiry into the various aspects of the sacred sciences so that an ever-deepening understanding of sacred revelation is obtained, the legacy of Christian wisdom handed down by our forefathers is more fully developed, the dialogue with our separated brethren and with non-Christians is fostered, and answers are given to questions arising from the development of doctrine.[35]

Therefore, ecclesiastical faculties should reappraise their own laws so that they can better promote the sacred sciences and those linked with

---

[34] Cf. Pius XI, Apostolic Constitution *Deus scientiarum Dominus*, May 24, 1931: *A.A.S.* 23 (1931), pp. 245-7.

[35] Cf. Pius XII, Encyclical Letter *Humani generis*, Aug. 12, 1950: *A.A.S.* 42 (1950), pp. 568f., 578; Paul VI, Encyclical Letter *Ecclesiam Suam*, part III, Aug. 6, 1964: *A.A.S.* 56 (1964), pp. 637-59; Vatican Council II, *Decree on Ecumenism*, November 21, 1964: *A.A.S.* 57 (1965), pp. 90-107.

them and, by employing up-to-date methods and aids, lead their students to more penetrating inquiry.

12. Cooperation is the order of the day. It increases more and more to supply the demand on a diocesan, national and international level. Since it is altogether necessary in scholastic matters, every means should be employed to foster suitable cooperation among Catholic schools, and between these and other schools that collaboration should be developed which the good of all mankind requires.[36]

From greater coordination and cooperative endeavor greater fruits will be derived, particularly in the area of academic institutions. Therefore, in every university let the various faculties work mutually to this end, insofar as their goal will permit. In addition, let the universities also endeavor to work together by promoting international gatherings, by sharing scientific inquiries with one another, by communicating their discoveries to one another, by having exchange of professors for a time and by promoting all else that is conducive to greater assistance.

CONCLUSION

The sacred Synod earnestly entreats young people themselves to become aware of the importance of the work of education and to prepare themselves to take it up, especially where, because of a shortage of teachers, the education of youth is in jeopardy.

---

[36] Cf. John XXIII, Encyclical Letter *Pacem in terris,* April 11, 1963: *A.A.S.* 55 (1963), p. 284 and elsewhere.

This same sacred Synod, while professing its gratitude to the priests, the religious men and women, and the laity who by their evangelical self-dedication are devoted to the noble work of education and of schools of every type and level, exhorts them to persevere generously in the work they have undertaken and, imbuing their students with the spirit of Christ, to strive to excel in pedagogy and the pursuit of knowledge in such a way that they not merely advance the internal renewal of the Church but preserve and enhance her beneficent influence upon today's world, especially the intellectual world.

* * *

Each and every point stated in this Declaration has satisfied the fathers of the sacred Council. And we, by the authority bestowed on us by Christ, together with the venerable fathers, approve it in the Holy Spirit, we decree it and we enact it; and we order the promulgation, to God's glory, of what has been enacted synodically.

Rome, in St. Peter's Basilica, October 28, 1965

Paul, Bishop of the Catholic Church
(The Fathers' signatures follow)

Study-Club Questions

1. Why must the Church be concerned with the whole of man's life, even the secular part of it?
2. Do all Christians have a right to a Christian education? What is a Christian education?

3. Who are the primary and principal educators of children? Who are the secondary educators? What is the place of the P.T.A. or the School and Home Association?

4. What is the role of civil society in education? How is civil society distinguished from society in general or "We-the-People"?

5. What is the role of the Church in education? of lay school boards?

6. Briefly discuss the value of catechetical instructions.

7. Briefly discuss the value of schools mentioned in n. 5.

8. Mention three harmful effects of monopoly in education.

9. How can Catholic schools aid in the fulfillment of the mission of the People of God and foster the dialogue between the Church and mankind?

10. What are the qualifications necessary to become a good Christian teacher? What is to be said of the vocation of a teacher in the public schools?

11. What should Catholic colleges and universities do to insure a deeper realization of the harmony of faith and science?

12. What does the Church expect from the faculties of sacred sciences?

13. What can you do not merely to advance the internal renewal of the Church but also to preserve and enhance its beneficent influence upon today's world, especially the intellectual world?

14. All Christians should assist in fostering the education of the young in society. Explain.

15. Mention and briefly discuss three important principles of Christian education contained in this Declaration.

16. Are parishes child-centered? Give evidence pro and con.

Results of Ballots on Schema on Christian Education
October 13 and 14, 1965

Vote		Voting	Placet	Non-Placet	Void
No. 1	Preface	2202	2117	85	
No. 2	Universal Right to Education	2194	2098	96	2
No. 3	Right to Christian Education	2181	2105	76	3
No. 4	Authors of Education	2120	2007	111	5
No. 5	Various Aids to Education	2108	2020	85	3
No. 6	Importance of Schools	2088	2000	83	5
No. 7	(Oct. 14) Duties and Rights of Parents .	2063	1961	99	3
No. 8	Religious Education in All Schools	2040	1956	79	5
No. 9	The Catholic Schools	2083	1977	102	4
No. 10	Different Types of Catholic Schools ...	2187	2068	116	3
No. 11	Catholic Colleges and Universities	2180	2043	132	5
No. 12	Faculties of Sacred Sciences	2184	2095	87	2
No. 13	Coordination of Schools and Conclusion .	2181	2079	100	2
No. 14	(on the entire schema)	2096	1912	183	1
	Final Ballot October 28, 1965	2,325	2,290	35	0

Appendix

INTERVENTION OF THE MOST REVEREND JOHN P. CODY, D.D.
ARCHBISHOP OF NEW ORLEANS
NOVEMBER 17, 1964

I speak in the name of the bishops of the United States of America, and also in the name of many bishops who work in the mission fields, and also as president of the association which is called the *National Catholic Education Association*. . . .

Since the question of Catholic education is so difficult and so complicated, especially in our times, on account of a certain evolution in the methods of teaching, both because of the human element and because of technical systems, the Commission has wisely suggested that after the acceptance of the present schema as a *Magna Carta* of Christian education, a post-conciliar Commission examine more broadly and more exactly all aspects of the problem. It is certain that this cannot happen in a few weeks or even a few months, and it must not be done by a post-conciliar Commission "a priori"; but first the various problems must be treated by episcopal conferences in each nation—with the help of various experts, either religious or lay—which must produce a certain program according to the principles established by the Declaration; it must then be submitted to the post-conciliar Commission for the purpose of coordination with the diverse programs of other nations.

Let me say that such a method of procedure seems

the best, both on account of the present shortage of time and on account of the complexity of the problems which need accurate study. Therefore, when it has been approved, the Declaration will offer the opportunity to all the bishops to examine the serious problem of education better and more at ease, in the light of the special conditions of each nation, and there to give suggestions which appear more useful for the solving of questions, afterwards to be examined by a post-conciliar Commission which will represent every episcopate.

Two questions especially occupy the minds of the heads of state: namely, defense and education. On the one side, there are those who, always fearful that war will break out, invest huge sums of money in the building of armaments; on the other side, however, since citizens are continually increasing in number, governments are compelled to build in greater numbers every day classrooms for students, universities, etc. The Church indeed, following the example of her divine Founder, always and efficaciously has exercised her office of teaching; however, nothing seems more useful to me now—especially if we heed the pastoral and the ecumenical spirit of the Council—than the approval of this Declaration which brilliantly demonstrates to the whole world the desire of the Church to cooperate, either nationally or internationally, in solving such grave problems of our times. For only if men are thoroughly instructed can they understand the difficulties of others, know well the desires and the aspirations of peoples, and foster their own good and indeed that of society, care for and promote it.

It seems to me moreover that Vatican Council II cannot deny approval to this Declaration which is so closely connected with the schemata already examined in this Council. For education is intimately connected with the schemata of *The Church in the Modern World, The Apostolate of the Laity, The Missionary Activity of the Church,* etc. If the Council does not act on Catholic education, there is no doubt that this will be a cause of great surprise and sorrow, since the principles pertinent to Catholic education are the foundation of the previously mentioned schemata and also of the apostolic mission and of the sanctifying Church in the whole world.

It is also proper to note that if the Council does nothing on Catholic education, it will bring certainly serious offense to innumerable lay Catholics who, not rarely, with great sacrifice generously sustain the Church in the exercise of her magisterial office, whether in Catholic universities or in primary schools, both parochial and abbatial, in secondary schools and colleges, which schools indeed have often been built by the Christian people not without tears or blood.

If we do not speak about Catholic education, Venerable Fathers, how can we join ranks with the many priests, religious, sisters and laity, daily increasing in number, who expend their energy generously for Catholic education? Our Declaration, accurately worked out by the Commission, will spur the souls of the laity to the assistance and defense of the Catholic schools; it will be a consolation and a solace to the priests, religious and laity who not rarely think that their apostolate is not sufficiently esteemed; it will be an incentive to the lay teachers whose help daily more and more we need in our schools; and this Declaration will finally be a solemn confirmation that the Church of our time, perhaps more than ever before, wishes to fulfill the divine mandate to "teach all nations".

Pardon me, Venerable Fathers, if I dare to mention the United States of America. For the Declaration approved by the Council will bring sincere joy to our 45 million Catholics who support 13,655 Catholic schools, which receive $10\frac{1}{2}$ million students in every grade of education directed by 191,126 priests, brothers, sisters and lay teachers.

The Declaration, which urges the building of Catholic schools wherever possible, will be of great assistance to the missionary activity of the Church. Lay teachers, whose help we need in order that many of our schools may live and flourish, priests, brothers and sisters would feel that they are indeed participants in the apostolic mission of the Church and provident cooperators of the bishops, as indeed it is stated in the *Decree on the Pastoral Office of Bishops in the Church:* "Bishops must see to it that they use the various means which are at hand to announce Christian doctrine in today's world, to wit, preaching and catechetical instruction which indeed always hold the principal place, but also the teaching of doctrine in the schools, in academies, conferences, etc., by which it is entirely fitting that the Gospel of Christ be announced."

Venerable Brothers, having heard the reasons given by His Excellency, the Relator, for the preference of this Declaration over the propositions which had been prepared before, and having before our eyes the importance of the question of Catholic education in the world of our time, I make bold to suggest that the Declaration produced by the Commission on Seminary Studies and Catholic Education be accepted by the Fathers, since it seems a solid basis for the happy exercise of the pastoral office so very often desired by this Council.

INTERVENTION OF AUXILIARY BISHOP JAMES MALONE YOUNGSTOWN, OHIO

Within the limits of its reduced form, this *Declaratio* on Christian education *placet*. All will concede that the *Declaratio* must be amplified, enlarged upon and expanded into a full document, as the Commission which drew up the schema suggests. Thus we suggest a fundamental proposition to undergird and to support our treatment of education: namely, that a *clear and explicit distinction* be elucidated *between society itself and the State or government* which is society's political arm or instrument.

It is not sufficient simply to affirm the rights of the Church in education, to proclaim the rights of the family, to delineate the rights of the State and its correlative duties. *It is equally necessary to give the reasons why* these rights and corresponding duties are what they are, to present both a theological and philosophical basis for the claims we make, and to fashion a coherent synthesis that makes sense not only to our own people but to all men of goodwill.

Our document justly affirms the rights of parents to choose the schools they wish for their children and their right to equal treatment under the laws of a nation in the matter of education; it equally rejects all monopoly of education as contrary to these parental rights. But the schema must go deeper and put into perspective the *delicate and complex relationships among all those agents with rights in education:* Church, State, family, private associations, schools, teachers and administrators, and the students themselves. The respective relationships put into focus in modern times by Pope Pius XI in his great encyclical on education, *Divini Illius Magistri,* must be developed further. We cannot rest our case simply on the affirmation of rights.

The school is not *simpliciter* the extension of the home or family; the teachers are not *simpliciter* the delegates of the parents or even of the Church. Neither is the school *simpliciter* the agent, much less the servant, of the State. Each agent in education has a proper and legitimate interest in the education of its children, but each from its own point of view and within the limits of its own competence.

Consequently, the full schema must include the fundamental distinction between society itself and the State. Society is a social concept which describes the community itself; society means "the people", or, as we say in English, "We the People", whereas in contrast the State is a political concept, much narrower in meaning. The State or the government is an instrument of society, the political arm of society, and its functions and specific duties must be determined by the consent of the people, *i.e.,* by society itself. Society then must be distinguished from the State or government precisely because it is not coterminous with it either in extension or in fundamental rights.

Contrary to some prevalent theories of the State, the government is not and must not become the master of the people, but rather its servant. In the field of education, the government must not be the official teacher and arbiter of religion, science, art, literature, music or culture. Rather, the State must be the servant of the expressed will and consent of the people with its unquestioned right to see to it that its citizens are fully equipped to fulfill their obligations as citizens and members of the body politic within the field of its proper competence.

Having made this fundamental point, the schema may then proceed to the general principles in education which concern man in the exercise of his highest faculties and in his dignity as a free person. The right of a family to equal treatment under the laws of a State or nation, the repudiation of all monopoly in education as an offense against the dignity of a parent to choose the school he wishes for his children, the right of equal justice in relationship to government subsidies in pluralistic societies, and the duties of the Church and the State alike to foster and assist parents in their task and duty will be brought into clearer focus.

The confusion in education today in most countries of the world, whether of the Occident or Orient, stems largely from a confusion of the bases upon which each agent in education vindicates its rights and duties. *The theory of State monopoly in education is based upon the total identification of society and the State.* We cannot answer that monopoly with a theory of family monopoly, or Church monopoly, in the 20th century.

This basic distinction between the people and its political arm, the State, will go a long way toward clearing up this confusion in the field of education.

We plead therefore for the freedom of man in the field of education and indeed as a prime test of the freedom of religion. *Dixi.*

INTERVENTION OF FRANCIS CARDINAL SPELLMAN
ARCHBISHOP OF NEW YORK

In accord with the purpose of this schema as is noted in the *proemium* itself, namely, to set forth "certain fundamental principles" on Christian education, we wish to say how excellently the Commission has attained this purpose.

I propose one verbal emendation so that the intention of the Council may be more clearly apparent from the text.

The direct intention of the schema is to affirm the rights of children and their parents, and not necessarily to seek money from the public treasury for religious schools. In many nations, for historic, sociological and political reasons, the question of the support of schools is a difficult and complicated one. Therefore, I propose the following emendation to be added to paragraph four on page 12 of the *Declaratio:*

"Parents should be free to choose the schools they wish for their children. They should not in consequence of their choice be subject to unjust economic burdens which would infringe upon this freedom of choice. Since it is the function of the State to facilitate civil freedoms, justice and equity demand that a due measure of public aid be available to parents in support of the schools they select for their children.

"Moreover, if these schools serve the public purpose of popular education, the fact that they may be religious in their orientation should not exclude them from a rightful measure of public support."

I propose this emendation so that the intention of the Council may be more clearly apparent, and accordingly I hope that useless quarrels over the words of the schema may be avoided in the future.

There remains, however, a more fundamental question. Is it really possible that this Council, or some post-conciliar Commission, or a Commission for the Revision of the Code of Canon Law, could recommend norms which will apply the fundamental principles to all the actual problems of Catholic schools and Christian education? In my opinion, considering the variety of schools from place to place with a consequent diversity of problems, no Commission can decide all the particular norms for the whole world or give definitive answers to the schools of all nations and their problems.

Therefore, I commend the Commission warmly for proposing a practical solution in the *proemium,* namely, the establishing of a special post-conciliar Commission to study further the intricate problems of Christian education. This Commission must not only have representation from the major areas of the world, but have truly expert members from all phases of education as well and include laymen along with priests and religious men and women. I commend the suggestion also that the practical applications of these general principles be placed in the hands of the conferences of bishops around the world in accord with the instructions of the Holy See.

Therefore, this Declaration, with some changes in expression, merits in my opinion a vote of *placet. Dixi.*

STATEMENT OF JOSEPH CARDINAL RITTER
ARCHBISHOP OF SAINT LOUIS
RELEASED TO PRESS ON NOVEMBER 18, 1964

The *Declaration on Christian Education* is very pleasing to me. The importance of the subject of Christian education can scarcely be exaggerated, since it involves the command of Christ to go forth and teach all nations. The subject itself, as is quite evident, deserves a much fuller treatment than was possible in the Declaration.

Not only is the subject itself a very complex one, involving a theology of education, a philosophy of education, and indeed special professional competence in the field of schools and universities, but it is made more complex by reason of its universal worldwide importance and interest. No statement in detail could possibly be applicable to all countries or even almost all countries with their diverse cultures, standards of living, and legal status for schools and the Church herself. Of particular moment in complicating the problems of such a document is the relationship of Church and State in each country, a delicate matter better solved country by country. Indeed, the school question with its diverse ramifications has become in many States the special practical test, the *cause celebre,* in the matter of the relationships between the Church and the State, between citizens and their government, between families and the society in which they live.

Rightly then does the Declaration call for a postconciliar *ad hoc* committee to make the necessary surveys and research in a professional manner in order to produce a document on education not only worthy of the Council but of real and genuine value to men of goodwill everywhere. The Commission rightly and laudably has eschewed a facile solution by compromise which would fit no country, help no nation, or be of real value to any people, and indeed might even compromise the very freedom of education which all men of goodwill desire. This post-conciliar *ad hoc* committee, if approved, deserves not only the support of the bishops but their cooperation in the research that they will make as a basis for a document suitable to our Vatican Council. I wish to affirm my wholehearted support for this solution proposed by the Commission on Schools and Universities. Also, the Commission proposes to leave to Episcopal Conferences themselves the specific application of the questions of Christian education in their own countries. This is certainly worthy of praise for the reasons I have already mentioned above.

I. It is noteworthy that the title of this Declaration has been changed from *De scholis catholicis* to *De educatione christiana,* a much wider term. The Catholic school is not and must not be the only concern of the Church. Most of the Catholic children and students in the world are in State schools and must be in fact the object of the solicitude of the Church, the family, and especially the teachers in these schools for their religious education.

This Synod should give a ringing endorsement to the work, particularly of the devoted laity, of Christian education as effected by the Confraternity of Christian Doctrine, the Schools of Religion, the Newman Foundations, the Young Christian Students, and similar organizations around the world devoted to the religious education of students not receiving formal religious education in State or secular or neutrally religious schools.

II. Rightly does the *Declaratio* affirm the freedom of parents to choose the schools they wish for their children. However, freedom must extend not only to the choice of schools but to the schools themselves. Within their own walls the Catholic schools must be models of Christian freedom in their administration, their teaching, and particularly in the interpersonal relationships among teachers, pupils and parents.

The matter extends too to the pursuit of learning. Often have we heard in the aula of the unity of the Church, of the unity of the people and family of God; there is also a unity of truth. Truth is one, integral and whole because, ultimately, with its source in the one God, truth cannot and does not in fact contradict itself. Consequently, our schools and their professors and students must pursue the truth boldly and freely without fear, confident that the truth they seek is none other than Christ who described himself as the Way, the Truth and the Life, that the truth they seek is the truth which the Sacred Scriptures declare will make us free.

Therefore, Catholic schools and colleges and universities must not only be free from unjust external coaction and coercion but must be models of Christian freedom within their own walls.

III. Our document on Christian education must emphasize that the Catholic schools do not exist to serve narrow sectarian purposes, or to protect selfish interests of the Church as if they were weapons of defense, or to shield boys and girls from the marketplace (forum) and public life. Rather, they stand as an expression of the free choice and liberal sacrifice not only of parents but of priests, the religious and devoted laymen and laywomen, for God and for country as well as for the families and the Church herself. Catholic schools indeed are, and of their very nature must be, of substantial benefit to the entire community where they serve and to society itself. Otherwise they would stand self-condemned and be unworthy of the title "Catholic".

CONCLUSION:

I warmly approve the solutions proposed in the *Declaratio* for a fuller schema and urge you, Venerable Brothers, to accord it a *placet* vote. *Dixi.**

Intervention of Bishop Hugh A. Donohoe Stockton, California

The *Declaration on Christian Education* is quite acceptable. A much fuller treatment is necessary, however, and the proposal of the Commission for a special *ad hoc* committee after the Council to draw up a truly professional document is also acceptable.

I. As stated in paragraph 4, parents do have the primary and inalienable right to choose the schools they wish for their sons and daughters. Furthermore, since parents are also citizens, they are entitled to equal and equitable treatment in this choice of schools under the laws of their country and do not at all forfeit their right by reason of the religion they profess or the type of school they choose for their children. Similarly, as the State and government must, the Catholic Church too stands willing to help parents fulfill their obligations in education.

However, in her zeal to assist the family, the Church must not forget the schools themselves. It is not at all sufficient to put the label "Catholic" upon a school, its administration and teaching corps; it is equally necessary that *the mark of excellence* be the goal and first purpose of the school, its administration and teaching staff. The Catholic Church must not be mesmerized by the mere numbers of schools or of children in them, but strive to conduct schools of *superior character and excellence*. Quality of education must never be sacrificed to

---

* Note: Cardinal Ritter used a somewhat different text in his oral intervention in the Council.

quantity or *to the tyranny of numbers.* Achievement is not necessarily proved by statistics.

In the same vein, the schools of the Church are *not defensive weapons* existing to shelter and protect children from the world and the marketplace like so many hothouse plants. Rather, these schools serve the family and children precisely *by preparing students to take their rightful place in the world,* to be *witnesses to Christ* not only without fear and with confidence, but as well *with intelligence and knowledge.*

Pope John XXIII, in *Pacem in terris,* par. 153, noted that often there is an inconsistency between religious faith in believers and their activity in the temporal sphere, due in great part to a lack of solid Christian education. Too often, he said, there is *no proportion between scientific training and religious instruction.* Therefore, it is clear that the Church on the one hand, *when she undertakes to conduct schools,* does so with a *dedication to excellence in all branches of learning,* not simply religion, and, on the other, when she undertakes *the religious education of those not in Church schools, does so with the same dedication to excellence.*

II. The Declaration speaks of the Catholic schools as *a true apostolate.* Would it not be better to expand this idea to include *all* schools, whether conducted by the Church, or by the State, or by private associations? And for whom are schools an apostolate? Surely not only for priests and the religious but *for the laity as well,* most especially those devoted laymen and laywomen who are teachers in State-conducted and other schools. Most of the Catholic children and students in the world are in State schools and must be the object of this true apostolate, especially by their teachers.

III. If we are to speak of parental rights and lay participation in schools, then we must be prepared *to accept the role of parents in the determination of policy in the Catholic schools;* we must be prepared as well to accept *laymen* not only as teachers but indeed *as administrators and presidents* of our Catholic institutions of learning.

IV. While we rightly insist on freedom for the schools chosen by parents, it is necessary that these schools *within their own walls* be models of Christian freedom. Proudly and confidently do we assert that our schools are dedicated to the truth, precisely as Christ called himself the Truth. We assert quite correctly that truth is one and whole, and cannot be found in contradiction to itself. Consequently, *there must be no fear in the pursuit of learning,* in the *pursuit of truth,* for *we seek the truth which the Gospel tells us will make us free.*

V. In our zeal for the rights of parents, we must not forget that there are other agents of education. We cannot fight monopoly by the State simply by asserting monopoly by the family. The schools do not belong *simply* to parents; neither do they belong *exclusively* to the Church, nor *exclusively* to the State, nor to the private associations which conduct them, nor, finally, *exclusively* to society itself. Each agent, according to its proper competence and within the limits of justice and equity, has its own proper interest in the education of students.

The schema should be *pastoral in tone,* evolving into a clear synthesis of the respective and reciprocal roles of all who are interested in education, including the educand himself.

CONCLUSION:

Christ told us that he is the Way, the Truth and the Life, and that the truth will make us free. *Boldly the schema should face this world challenge in Christian education in the spirit of disinterested service to family, nation and Church.*